**HER CHARGE OF RAPE SENT A MAN TO JAIL.
EIGHT YEARS LATER, SHE RECANTED.
CATHY WEBB TELLS HER OWN STORY . . .**

Here is the powerful story of a young girl's life of
lies and her remarkable journey to truth and re-
pentance. Learn how a sixteen-year-old girl de-
ceived a court of law, her family, and everyone
who knew her. Listen to the moving confession of
the woman who faced a nationwide controversy to
admit boldly: "I lied . . . That man is innocent."

_____

"The truths disclosed in FORGIVE ME will satisfy the
curious and the skeptics, as well as those who believe."
—**MOODY**

"If you can believe in the force of faith to change a person, you can believe Cathleen Crowell Webb's story."
—**NEW HAMPSHIRE SUNDAY NEWS**

"Were the story fiction, it would be compelling enough.
Its basis in fact . . . makes it an especially chilling read."
—**CHICAGO SUN-TIMES**

"The author, Marie Chapian, does a good job of setting
the scene of a small lie and watching it mushroom . . . It
is a book which, regardless of her (Cathy's) agenda and
Gary's innocence or guilt, gives readers an opportunity
to experience the trauma of a very painful childhood."
—**ROCHESTER POST-BULLETIN**

_____

Marie Chapian has written over 12 books, including STAYING HAPPY IN AN UNHAPPY
WORLD, GROWING CLOSER, and WHY DO
I DO WHAT I DON'T WANT TO DO? Her
bestselling book, FREE TO BE THIN, has over
600,000 copies in print.

FORGIVE ME

CATHLEEN CROWELL WEBB and MARIE CHAPIAN

BERKLEY BOOKS, NEW YORK

Scripture quotations in this book are taken from the King James Version of the Bible.
Quotations from *The Flame and the Flower* by Kathleen E. Woodiwiss, Avon Books, © 1972.
Quotations from *Sweet Savage Love* by Rosemary Rogers, Avon Books, © 1974.
Material quoted from the *Chicago Lawyer* © 1985 and used by permission.

This Berkley book contains the complete
text of the original hardcover edition.
It has been completely reset in a typeface
designed for easy reading, and was printed
from new film.

FORGIVE ME

A Berkley Book / published by arrangement with
Fleming H. Revell Company

PRINTING HISTORY
Fleming H. Revell edition published 1985
Berkley edition / October 1986

ISBN: 0-425-09436-7

A BERKLEY BOOK ® TM 757,375
Berkley Books are published by The Berkley Publishing Group,
200 Madison Avenue, New York, NY 10016.
The name "BERKLEY" and the stylized "B" with design
are trademarks belonging to Berkley Publishing Corporation.
PRINTED IN THE UNITED STATES OF AMERICA

CONTENTS

PART I

Jaffrey, New Hampshire
June 25, 1985

I pull into the rutted driveway at the side of an old two-story, wood frame house. A young woman is in the backyard with a hose filling a child's plastic pool with water. She's wearing a green pullover shirt, a denim skirt, and sandals. Her hair is straight and clean and she wears no makeup. I recognize her from the newspaper photos. This is Cathy Webb, the young woman I and millions of others have seen on TV and in the newspapers. Like everyone else who's heard the story, I'm wondering what she's like. What kind of woman could send an innocent man to prison for six years for a rape that she now says never happened?

She puts out her hand, but I ignore it and give her a hug. We go into the house, but not before she finishes filling the pool.

The room we enter is long and bare, except for a small, square wooden table in the center of it. At one end is a stove and refrigerator and alcove sink area, with another counter alcove along the wall. There is blue-and-white print wallpaper on the wall ("I hate it," she says) and natural oak floors and woodwork. One wall is brick; in front of it stands a wood-burning stove. The sparseness of the room is reminiscent of an earlier rural America.

We sit at the table while Andrew, age three, and Elizabeth, almost two, skitter back and forth across the floor with handfuls of Playskool parts. I glance into the porch behind me through the slightly opened door and it's filled with toys, stacks of them: dolls, a dollhouse, Playskool gas station, doll buggy, crib, wooden trucks, and a pile of stuffed animals. Elizabeth asks her mother for a cracker and Cathy lifts her to the high chair, settles her in it, and places a soda cracker on the tray for her. Andrew eats his while playing on the floor.

Talk begins with a discussion of Cathy's movie offers. She's had forty-one of them so far, according to what her lawyer has told her. All of this movie business, she reflects, is a real pain. Producers have even sent certified checks along with their contracts. She could have cashed checks for just her signature, but she sent the packages back immediately. [Later, I would find out that the Webbs were two months behind in their bills. And yet they were turning down hundreds of thousands of dollars.] She won't receive money for this book; the royalties from *Forgive Me* are going into a fund for Gary Dotson, the man she accused of raping her.

Cathy Webb is not pretentious. She doesn't even try to be charming. She's plain, almost prim, and acts as if she really doesn't give two hoots what anyone thinks of her. I ask what she wants to say in the book. She says, "I want people to know how the Lord can change a person. How He can change a person's heart. The media never expressed that. They made me look like a real jerk." She pours herself a glass of lemonade. I have a glass of ice water. The conversation turns to the case, Gary Dotson, Warren Lupel (Dotson's lawyer), the clemency hearing, the "Today" show. I have the feeling she's sizing me up.

"Why don't people think you're telling the truth?" I ask.

"Because they can't understand. They don't know what it's like to experience the convicting presence of God. I never would have come forward out of my own sense of conscience. I would have gone on lying forever. I was too scared to tell the truth.''

"You must have lied to yourself, too. What lie did you tell yourself?"

"That I had no choice but to bury the truth, that there was nothing else I could do. I really believed that. See, I believed at the time it happened there was nothing I could do but go along with the lie because it kept building and building. Afterward I just refused to think about it. I snuffed it out of my mind."

"But God didn't snuff it out of His mind, is that right?"

"Yes, that's right."

Elizabeth finishes her cracker and is ready to be released from the high chair. Cathy lifts her out and the baby wraps her legs around her mother's waist. "Do you get much mail about all this?" I ask.

"Oh, yes, support from all over the world. There have been articles in newspapers in Singapore, Italy, Australia, New Zealand, England, even Japan . . . I get lots of mail and I still haven't answered it all." Does she answer her mail by hand? Yes, she does. She doesn't have a typewriter.

Before long the door opens and David Webb, Cathy's husband, enters the room. He's twenty-five years old, with the muscular build and broad shoulders of a man who is an ironworker by trade. He's wearing a T-shirt and jeans. He got off work early today. The talk becomes centered on lunch—should we go out to eat or order something to take home? We decide to go out to a restaurant.

We ride in their Ford van ("two hundred thousand miles on this thing, imagine!") to a restaurant in Peterborough. Elizabeth and Andrew are strapped in their seat belts behind me, chattering to me. Cathy has turned sideways in her seat to talk. She's warmer now; smiles even.

"What do you like best about your life now?" I ask.

"My family," she answers without a pause.

"What's the best thing about living in New Hampshire?"

"Being here with my family."

We drive along a winding forested road, through groves of pine, birch, and conifers, up twisted hills of elm and oak. Behind are the Monadnock Mountains, blazing green and orange in the sun. "You ought to see it here in autumn," Cathy says, "it's gorgeous."

At the restaurant, heads turn as she passes; the people know who she is. Her picture has been on the front pages of newspapers for the last two and a half months. They don't greet her or give any sign of recognition —they just turn to stare and then quickly turn back again, like those little wooden figures in German clocks that come out on the hour, turning and then popping back inside. I mention that people are looking at her and she comments, "The people of New England are different from people anywhere else. In Chicago at the time of the clemency hearing, for example, people came up to me on the street and started talking to me as though they knew me. You know, they'd say things like, 'I think you're telling the truth, keep your chin up,' or, 'How could you do such a terrible thing to another human being?' But people here in New England just look. They don't want to intrude unless it's to say something nice. Very proper. I guess maybe they go home and talk behind closed doors."

"Besides," David adds, "we'll never really be accepted here anyhow because we aren't Yankees—maybe our kids will be."

The waiter approaches, staring at Cathy. "Hello folks, the special today is . . ." We order sandwiches, salads, sodas, and water. I ask David to explain what he meant by *Yankee*.

"Well, you've got to be born in New England to be considered a Yankee. Like a woman I met who was bragging how she was a Yankee, born right in Rindge sixty-two years ago and lived here all her life. I thought her husband was a Yankee, too, but she frowned and told me in no uncertain terms that her husband was *not* a Yankee. He was from Pennsylvania. He had only lived in Rindge fifty years. He was no Yankee. So you see, an outsider is always an outsider to a Yankee.''

''Do you think the people here would respond differently to you now if you were a native New Englander, a Yankee?''

''No, they're very proper and good people here. They'll stare only if they think you won't notice. Not like in New York City where they stared, took our pictures, followed us, and even tried to get in the cab with us. It's different here.''

The food arrives and I'm looking for clues, signs, indications to tell me what kind of person Cathy is. I'm evaluating. Her attention is on the children, cutting their food, wiping their mouths. I get the feeling both she and David mistrust media people.

''When I came forward I never thought that people wouldn't believe me,'' she says to no one in particular.

I ask how David has held up through the past couple of months of hearings and all the attention from the media. ''Well, I missed a lot of work. And if I don't work I don't get paid, so it's not easy. We're behind. I just wanted to get Dotson out of jail and go on with life. That's all we've thought about.''

Cathy keeps her eyes on Andrew, who's playing with his lettuce. ''I came forward thinking if I told the truth and if the man was still in jail, he would get out of jail. I didn't even remember his name. I expected to confess and then probably be put in jail myself.''

How could so many news reporters have missed what I was seeing right now—the clear, unclouded eyes of a broken and vulnerable human being whose life was no longer hers? Not much that I had read of the Webb-Dotson case convinced me Cathy Webb was telling the truth or that she wasn't a little off her rocker.

In the hours I spent with Cathy that day I searched for symbols liars can't hide, body language that spoke of something more than self-consciousness, that showed denial and lying. I looked for inconsistencies in her testimony. I waited for some of the overt signals I would recognize immediately: blinking of the eyes, hands on the face, stretching the neck, rubbing the eyes, looking away, clearing the throat, touching the nose. I looked for clusters, symbols, behaviors that would speak louder than words . . . yet I saw none of these.

One thing puzzled me: She didn't seem to care whether or not I liked her. She did not try to impress me. I am not accustomed to this behavior, especially among Christians who are usually extremely warm and friendly toward one another.

David wants to show me one of the most beautiful spots in the area, the top of Pak Monadnock Point. We drive up a twisted road that must be torture in the winter, and park at the crest where giant forested canyons, gouged out of granite cliffs, reach as far as the eye can see, peaking, tumbling, arching, and engraving their verdant summer hue against the sky, which now seems shrunken. (The little boy, Andrew, pauses and stares at the scene before him. Wide-eyed, he exclaims, "Mommy, look what God made!")

Cathy and I walk away from David and the kids to talk. The mountain breeze encircles us and there, high above the rest of the world, the coolly distant person I met earlier that day fades slowly as a new person takes her place: one who talks nonstop, holding nothing back. It's fitting, I observe, that we're standing on a crest such as this; I let down my own guard to allow myself to see her, hear her, and know her. The defenses slowly bend and break and I believe we may be friends. She talks about her mother first, and tells a little about her early years. She's telling me facts, as well as how she felt. "I went to live with an older woman I called 'Aunt Nellie,' though she was no relation. I used to lie to please her . . . I lied all the time as I got older. . . ." She tells me how she met David at a bus stop after school, about the goals she had as a teenager to become an independent and successful businesswoman, and how all that has changed. She talks of her foster parents, Bernie and

Carol Smith, and finally she speaks of her father. "It looks as if I've lost my real father for good, although I've never really had him. His wife was so upset at the *People* magazine article, I heard she was supposed to have had some sort of breakdown. Uncle Bill, the one I've always loved like a real father—he raised me more or less—he won't talk to me now either. . . ."

You can tell what things are most important by the things a person saves until last to say. Our conversation throughout the day has centered on her incredible "story in the news," but that is almost incidental now. She talks on and on and words such as *alone* and *unhappy* and *lie* are repeated. One time she even says *hate* when she speaks of her father, whom she once adored.

She smiles. "I'm a Christian now, though, and I'm learning to deal with these feelings. I've really changed —not because of *my* abilities or anything, but because the Lord has given me different desires and changed me from the inside out."

She asks if I saw the article in *People* magazine. Yes, I had. "Well, a complete story can't be written in a couple of pages. The interviewer did the best she could with limited time and space, but too much was missing. Because of that, I've lost people who were important in my life. You know, it's funny, because all my life I wanted a real family and that's the very thing I could never have. You want to know what my recanting has done to me personally? I'll tell you. I can't go anywhere or do anything without being labeled now, and I'm not labeled for something good or wonderful. Who wants to be known for what's shameful? Putting an innocent man in prison for six years isn't something to be proud of. Promiscuous sex isn't something I'm proud of. I've lost a kind of dignity, I guess. I've lost people. But you know something? I believe I have done what the Lord wanted me to do. I've obeyed Him."

"Are you totally relieved now?" I ask.

"No. I won't be until Gary Dotson receives a complete pardon. The State is still saying he's guilty. He's out of jail, but it's not acknowledged that he's innocent of committing a crime, which he is." She pauses. "I did that to him." A look of pain so great passes across her face that I turn my eyes away.

Back at their house I follow Cathy as she opens a makeshift wire gate and walks the children inside the yard. She's the kind of woman you see in the supermarket but don't really notice. The grass is spotted brown and there are no flowers. We climb the steps as a white ruffled curtain lifts and sways in the window. I hear the wingbeat of a single sparrow.

Later we sit in the bright living room, which is lined with windows on two sides. An oyster-colored Indian cotton sofa along the wall faces the windows, and beside it is an end table and lamp. There are two designer chairs in the corners of the room and a coffee table stands in front of the sofa. The oriental rug centered on the floor completes the decor. That's all—good taste, sparse, and safe.

Outside the window by the fence, a horse and pony slap flies with their tails. I wonder if it's a mother and her baby. Cathy tells me no, it's not, and she's reminded of mothers and babies in general. "Wait 'til you meet David's mother. She is a wonderful lady. David's mother is accepting, affectionate, makes a person feel at home. That's what I always wanted. Both of David's parents are loving and make you feel special, you know? Like at holidays, they don't have a lot of money to spend, but a person can feel so loved by them. That's what I always wanted in a family."

I ask her to tell me about her real parents and memories of her early childhood. She pauses. "Well, my mother was raised by her grandparents during her younger years, and I think she grew up in Chicago because that's where she met my father."

She tells me she was born in Worth, Illinois, a small town of twelve thousand people southwest of Chicago in Cook County, on June 26, 1961. "We lived on West

One hundred and third Place, but I don't really remember it very well.

"My parents knew each other as kids, and I always thought that was a neat time to meet the one you're going to marry.

"David and I met when we were in high school, you know. And my parents sort of grew up together, too, I guess. They were in the same clique. In fact, one childhood friend of my parents called John McLario, my lawyer, when all this stuff about my recantation came out in the media. He wanted to know if I was all right in the head. You see, my mother wasn't well for many years. And this man knew my parents when my mother started getting sick. Do you know that I never knew what was wrong with her? It was through that phone call I found out the name of the sickness my mother had all those years. After twenty years, I just found out two months ago that she was a schizophrenic. I guess this man wondered if I was a little nutsö, too. Well, John McLario thought that was pretty funny. He assured the caller I was quite normal and sane.

"Does it really sound so crazy that I came forward to right a wrong?"

Later, when I go over Cathy's parents' divorce papers, I notice they were married at Hamilton Air Force Base in California on September 30, 1950. "Wasn't your father in the navy?" I ask. "Yes, he was," Cathy tells me, and shows me a wallet-sized studio portrait she has kept most her life of her father as a young man in his sailor uniform.

"I adored my father. I was only four when my parents separated, but I can remember certain things before that time, even though they're cloudy. You know how childhood memories are. But I remember those days because, you see, when I was put in a foster home, I wanted to hold on to my "real" home. I thought about it all the time—I couldn't dare forget. I believed my father would come back for me one day."

As she speaks, a picture of a child forms in my mind:

I see her materializing while Cathy talks, adds, refines.
As I listen the picture gets clearer: she's a blond-haired
child, a moon-eyed girl with fragile pale porcelain skin.
She bears a strong resemblance to Cathy's own daughter
now. I can see this little girl, playing with her dolls as
little girls do, but she is different from other little girls.
The crucial stage of child development, the one where
trust is formed, has been interrupted before it has a
chance to build or grow. She's someone's little girl,
almost four years old, and she doesn't know what's
happening to her. I invite this little girl to take the place
of the adult in the room with me now. I can imagine her,
as she talks to me, bouncing on an overstuffed chair in
her living room at 103rd Place in Worth, Illinois.

It's 1964. . . .

1

Worth, Illinois
1964

SHE IS THREE years old and lives in a house made of bricks. She likes to bounce on the puffy chairs in the living room with her Cuddly Dudley doll. Mother is there; she's in her room in bed now, crying. When the child asks Mother why she's crying, she stops. She doesn't want her children to see her that way. She tries to stay cheerful, be a good mother, but it's so hard sometimes. One activity her little girl always seems to enjoy is brushing her mother's hair, so Mommy puts a tissue to her nose and asks the child if she'd like to brush her hair.

The little girl's brothers are outside playing—they always get to go outside. They can do so many things she isn't allowed to do. Donnie is ten years older than her, and Stevie is eight years older. Next to Mommy and Daddy, she loves them best in the world.

Her mother has pretty brown hair, like the color of Hershey's Kisses. Mother tells her she's a good girl. Mother loves to hug her little girl, loves to stroke her hair, touch her arm, hold her hand. "I love you so much," Mother tells her. "Oh, Mommy, I love you, too!"

Sometimes the child cries when Mommy cries. But what's worst of all is when Mommy pulls down the shades and locks the doors tight; oh, then the child is so afraid. Mother's face is very angry. Maybe it was the little girl's fault. Mother stomps her anger out on the floor and her slippers flap on her feet. She tells the little girl to stop crying and to play with her Cuddly Dudley doll.

The little girl knows something is terribly wrong. It's dark and scary with the drapes and curtains drawn. She cries for her daddy.

Then there's a rattling at the door. Mommy says not to move. But then there's the doorbell, the pounding, and Daddy's voice calling. "It's Daddy," she tells her mother. But Mother is angry and tells her to shush.

"What's wrong, Mommy? What's wrong?"

Daddy wants to come in. Why won't she let him in? Then he's at the kitchen door and the child rushes to open it for him, but Mommy gets there first. Her hand folds over the small one. "No, don't do that." So many words, bad words. She doesn't want to hear them. Pounding. Pounding. Then he's gone and they're locked inside alone. The little girl is sure it's all her fault.

Mother shakes and cries again. Fourteen years they've been married, not without trials, but now these episodes. Oh, it's hard. The little girl can't understand who's bad, who's good. Her mother doesn't trust anyone and says such terrible things.

Some days Mommy huddles in a corner of the kitchen with her robe wrapped tightly around her body, staring at the door and walls as if something bad was going to come through and get her. But then Daddy comes home and the drapes are open. Sunlight fills the kitchen.

At night Daddy tucks his daughter in and kisses her and says, "Good night, Princess." One night she tells him she doesn't like the Mafia one bit.

He looks sick, as if he swallowed something too big.

What was his Princess talking about?

Cathy tells him Mommy says the Mafia is coming to

get her. Then his face is full of shadows; he slumps on the bed. She had hoped he would make things all better, kiss her and tell her not to worry, nothing can hurt her—but he doesn't.

Other bad things are coming to get Mommy, she says: the Communists dressed as bus drivers, policemen, newspaper reporters, or nurses. Mother never knows when one might recognize her and take her away.

Mommy is never cross with her little girl—never spanks or yells at her. Mother's touch, though unsure and nervous, is always gentle, caring. She's like a bird, like a little sparrow in the yard.

The child can't understand what strange worries possess her mother or why she dreads things that aren't there. The Mafia isn't in the kitchen. Cathy looked! She was the only one there.

It is fun to eat her favorite snack, which Mother prepares in the shadowy kitchen. The child perches in a yellow high chair with her legs dangling down below the footrest while hungrily waiting for her bowl of brown sugar with water sprinkled on top. She loves that.

Donnie and Stevie are talking about Mommy going away again to Florida for another rest. The little girl begins to cry. Donnie comforts her and calls her "Squirt." He asks her what she'd like to do for fun.

"Eat ice cream," she says.

And so that's what they do. Donnie always makes her feel better. He is thin, and his pale skin is almost gray. He has soft moon eyes. Stevie has hair like Mother's and warm hazel eyes. Donnie and Stevie are good to Cathy. They are her family. She believes that's how it always will be. She believes her mother will be happy again; everything will be happy.

Donnie and Stevie play games and laugh and tell stories. It's lots of fun to be with them. She loves it when they take her along wherever they go, even if it is just to eat apples picked from a neighbor's tree.

Donnie likes to teach her things. "Here's how you write your name, Squirt; it's C-A-T-H-Y. Now you do it." But she's thinking about playing in the park. "Let's go swing, Donnie.'' He says okay.

One day she visits her mother in the cafeteria at the big hospital. Mommy's face is red and she looks sad. So very sad. The little girl cries when they take her away from her mother. ''When can Mommy come home?'' Daddy says when Mommy is well. She tells herself Mommy and Daddy will be happy then, and she won't be the cause of their troubles anymore.

Her father tells her to stop crying. He tells her she's spoiled. But she isn't spoiled, she argues. No, not her. That's for positive sure.

She doesn't want to make her daddy angry, and she's sorry for pulling the stick shift in the car. He was so angry. He told her she could have *killed* them! Oh, that's a terrible thing. She doesn't wet the bed anymore. She's a big girl.

She has a wish: she wishes people wouldn't get angry at her.

When Mother is gone the little girl looks in her closet to see if she's hiding, just playing a game. Sometimes Mommy does that. But now she is never there. Cathy likes to smell her mommy's clothes. She can smell her perfume and the smoke from her cigarettes. Daddy was very angry when Mommy went to the restaurant to look for him. She could hear them arguing in their bedroom. She thinks about that now when she sniffs Mommy's bathrobe, but it no longer smells like Mommy.

Then Mother comes home and everything isn't happy. The arguments are loud and bad, and Cathy is afraid. The fighting is louder than a thunderstorm; her parents are unaware of the small ears that can't escape their voices.

The family moves to an apartment building with an elevator. It makes the little girl very happy. But then Mommy and Daddy have a fight. When Daddy leaves, he is very angry. Cathy rushes after him to the elevator crying, and he turns around and tells her to go back to her mother. ''It's all my fault my daddy and mommy don't like each other anymore,'' she tells her Cuddly Dudley.

Daddy moves to a blue building on Lake Shore Drive. There are mountains of silver buildings all around and they twinkle at night like lots of eyes, but in the daytime they turn back into ordinary windows. Daddy makes eggs to eat every day. Cathy hates eggs. If she could live anywhere in the world, she would live where there wasn't one single egg. How can grown-ups eat something as awful as eggs?

Sometimes she's at Mommy's new house and sometimes she stays at Daddy's. "Why can't we have just one house, like we used to have?" That's what she wants to ask.

Donnie and Stevie tell ghost stories. They go to a neighbor's house and flick the lights on and off, then they come back and ask Cathy, "Did you see *that?* Those were *ghosts* in that house!" She asks Donnie, what does *spoiled* mean?

Donnie and Stevie take her places with them, but she's too heavy to carry. They figure out a way she won't run away when they take her to the beach with them. "You'll be safe," they tell her, "as long as you have this rope tied around you." They tie the other end of the rope to a garbage can. They really want her to understand. Stevie says, "Now you won't get run over or killed." She doesn't want to get killed. She doesn't want the ghosts to get her, either.

Stevie says Cathy has to take a bath but she won't take a bath unless he brings Mr. Puppet to the bathtub to sing songs to her. Mr. Puppet tells her she must take a bath because little girls who don't take baths turn into little piggies. Mr. Puppet is very happy when she takes her bath. He sings and claps his hands. Cathy loves Mr. Puppet and she loves Stevie.

It's raining today when Daddy comes to Mommy's house, and he screams again. He doesn't like it when his daughter eats brown sugar and water.

Daddy says Donnie and Stevie are in trouble. But she knows they are good boys because they love her. Does Daddy love her? She doesn't want him to be angry

because she pulled the stick shift in the car. He said she
could have *killed* them. She doesn't want him to be
angry because she wet his big bed on Lake Shore Drive,
either. Oh, she wishes people wouldn't get angry at her.
Mommy says she'll come and get her again when she is
able to.

A lady who calls herself a social worker gives Cathy
yellow Life Savers. She doesn't like that green smelly
gum that lawyer man in the black coat gave her. The
social worker asks her what she had for breakfast. It
must make her happy when the child tells her ice cream
because she writes it down in her book. Why do grown-
ups go away? Donnie and Stevie go away, too. Mr. Puppet doesn't talk if Stevie isn't there.

She gets to ride in Daddy's new car. They're going
visiting. The big trees make shadows like ghosts. She
doesn't like it when Daddy tells her she has to act like a
big girl because that means he's going away. And when
he goes away she's scared.

Last night when she was sleeping in her own bed
Cathy heard a sound nearby and woke up quickly. She
saw her brothers crawling out the window. "Don't tell
anyone," they whispered.

But wouldn't they take her along?

No, because she was going to a new place. She's there
now, sleeping in a new bed. There's a very old lady
there. She has giant arms and white hair. She makes
meatballs and biscuits. Will she be very angry if she
hears crying?

Cathy lies staring at the big trees out the window and
she thinks of slipping out to a peaceful place far, far
away, where adults don't scream at each other and she
won't have to cry. . . .

2

1965

CATHY'S FATHER BROUGHT her to Nellie Landers' house for dinner, he said. Dinner on the round Formica table amid the smells of meatballs and sauce and the faint drifting scent of camphor. Nellie was an old lady with sharp, darting eyes magnified by thick-lensed glasses. She was fat and kindly and held her large arms out to the child. "Come here, Cathy, and say hello to Aunt Nellie."

Once swallowed up in those moist, fleshy arms, released from her father's grip, Cathy had no way of knowing her world as someone's daughter had ended.

In the years to come she would replay the memories of those days before she went to Nellie's again and again—like the time her brothers tied her shoelaces together while she sat fussing in the high chair so she'd stop kicking. Was that just yesterday? She would pummel her mind to unlock the memories of the days when she was a daughter in a real family, with real parents and brothers of her own, when Stevie put on his puppet shows at the edge of the bathtub. Memories tended to drift away like smoke. The tenderness between a mother and her child would remain for Cathy a fantasy. It would confuse her, frighten her, knot her stomach. Where *was* that house in Worth, Illinois?

Why weren't Donnie and Stevie with her that day she went to dinner at Nellie's? Their faces were forever imprinted on the glass of a snow-smeared window, as was the memory of a father who held her on his lap, loved her, tickled her, and told her she was his Princess; yes, it *had* been that way once. But then it was over, snatched away for a plate of meatballs and a bowl of biscuits. The deeper part of her would forever be unfed, unquieted. Her mother was back in the hospital for a time, and was unable to care for her children. The boys stayed with their father, went to a private boarding school, were on their own, and then with their mother. But Cathy never was told or at least never understood.

"Aunt Nellie" the woman wanted to be called, even though she wasn't Cathy's aunt, or any relation whatsoever, for that matter; she was a friend of her mother's grandmother and known for her benevolence toward children, especially homeless or troubled ones. One of her foster sons, Bill, was middle-aged now but still lived with Nellie.

She was also known for her sharp-as-pins business and real estate acumen. She had been married more than once and had three sons, one of whom had been a policeman and was murdered. Nellie must have looked like the ideal answer to the dilemma facing Cathy's father. Actually, his real problem was that he was remarrying and Aunt Nellie was far more willing to house and feed Cathy than was his intended bride. Pat seemed older than Cathy's father. She was always finely dressed and smelled of thick, woodsy perfume that made Cathy's nostrils itch.

There was the time, Cathy remembered, in that restaurant when Donnie and Stevie wore pressed stiff shirts and funny crooked bow ties with their cowlicks slicked down. She was dressed in a prim ruffled dress Pat had bought for her. Her father excused himself from the table for a moment and the children watched as they thought they saw this charming lady become solidly cold. When her father returned to the table, so did the charm. Pat had bought Cathy pretty clothes and

Mary Jane shoes to show her off to her friends. But that time was short-lived and Cathy never had the chance to fit into Pat's life in any way whatsoever. There was a moment, Cathy recalled, when she thought Pat might care a little. That was when Pat patiently showed her how a little lady takes off her clothes when she hangs them up at night. "You pull a dress over your head, Cathy. You don't yank the arms out of the sleeves first because you might tear your pretty dress."

How or why the choice of Nellie Landers, an old woman in her twilight years who had long lost the touch of mothering, was made for Cathy, she never knew. She still doesn't know. When he took her to Nellie's house that night, her father told her he left her there for dinner, but he meant he left her for good.

The months went by and she cried for her daddy, her mommy, and her brothers. One day she even cried for her great-grandfather, who once or twice had held her on his lap, which drew a sigh out of the thin lips of Nellie Landers.

There were no shouting fights in this new house. Daylight wasn't hidden by drawn drapes. There weren't any mysterious dangers and scary shadows. Except for Cathy's occasional tearful episodes of asking where her daddy was and when he was coming to take her home, it must have appeared to Nellie that the child was adjusting fairly well. She told the social worker so. Nellie was caring for another foster child at the time, a ten-year-old retarded boy named Billy. "The two are getting along just fine," she informed the woman from the State.

Nellie was kind and sensitive those first years, and let Cathy know the very first week she arrived that baking cookies or making fudge in her kitchen could help remove the redness from a little girl's eyes and dry up the tear puddles from her face.

"Little girls' noses turn purple if they cry too much. Now you don't want a purple nose, do you?" (A loud wail of alarm.)

"All right, all right, then we'll have to bake some chocolate cookies, how does that sound?" (Sobs and nods.)

"Good. Now, are you any good at eating chocolate?" (Nods with a finger in mouth.)

"I thought so. Well, while we make our cookies, you can nibble on the chocolate, but just a tiny bit because—"

The child suddenly lost the sound of Nellie's voice and her finger dropped from her mouth. There in the cupboard, staring down at her, stood a familiar striped box of brown sugar. It could have been her mother standing there herself, and Cathy reacted with a burst of emotion that took Nellie by surprise.

Poor Nellie Landers, never to the day she died, understood why there had to always be, facing front, in plain view, a two-pound box of brown sugar in the cupboard.

If the girl cried, Aunt Nellie baked. Smells of cookies in the oven overtook the little house daily and the boy who slept in the bed next to Cathy must have thought the new girl brought a special cookie angel with her when she moved in.

3

1966

HER BEDTIME WAS 7:30. That meant *in* the bed with face and hands washed, teeth brushed ("Brush up and down, not sideways, child, didn't they ever teach you anything?"), tucked in, prayers said, and lights out. "Every child has to get at least twelve hours of sleep a night." On Friday nights Cathy was allowed to stay up later, so that's why on this particular night she was lying on the floor, chin cupped in her hands, watching TV. Beside her was Billy, the boy Nellie knew positively well was retarded, even if the State said he was normal in order to get him into a foster home. Aunt Nellie confided to her granddaughter, Carol, on the telephone, "Lord, anyone with only one eye and barely enough sense to catch a fly could see that boy's got a screw loose." Nellie's foster son Bill, whom she had raised since he was just a tot, lounged in the brown chair on the other side of the room. Nellie surveyed the group while a buxom red-haired actress on the screen told of her recent harrowing exploits in Africa.

"I never had a daughter," Nellie had been heard to say. Girls were harder than boys, always had been, always would be. Cathy's daddy had dropped her off without so much as a hairpin to call her own. Bill, sitting over there in the brown chair, had come to Nellie when he was a little boy. He came with his two brothers, but Bill had stayed the longest of them all. She glanced at the TV screen.

Bill chuckled at a joke. Billy picked up the cue and roared with laughter, rolling to one side. Cathy observed them curiously.

Nellie shifted her heavy body forward onto her right hip. Grunting, she pulled herself to the edge of the sofa. The girl followed her movements.

Nellie wished she hadn't sat on the sofa in the first place. Her own comfortable gray chair was within arm's distance. And then, at her side like a flash, was the child reaching for her. "Do you feel okay, Aunt Nellie? Can I help you?"

The old woman stared owl-eyed at the five-year-old girl.

"Yes, you can help Aunt Nellie to her chair." And so she did, pulling, tugging, and genuinely bracing herself for the weight of the giant dough woman. Where had she learned to lift an adult person this way? Nellie settled in, jiggling and joggling back and forth to the comfort of her gray chair, and the child returned to her position on the floor. Billy now rocked back and forth on his haunches, absorbed in the TV program.

Nellie ignored the program. She mused as she observed Cathy. She'd train her right, and the child would do fine. Nellie said in a low voice, "Cathy, go get Aunt Nellie a glass of water."

When the girl returned with the water, Nellie said, "Now you can go to bed," which she reluctantly but promptly did.

First the terror, then the nightmares in every crook of a strange new home, then the confusion, the mistrust. Unfamiliar people became Cathy's major caretakers, monoliths she would have hidden behind Mother's legs to keep from facing, if her mother had been there. Then came the hollow, lost feeling, the loneliness. The knowing you've lost something and are guilty. Finally came the questions. The giants of the adult world who made

choices for her didn't explain what went wrong. Was
she responsible for being here because she was naughty
in her real home? Was she being punished? Was it
because she wet the bed that night on Lake Shore Drive?
And she did playfully yank the steering wheel, after all,
when her father was driving.

She had heard her mother say she couldn't take it any
longer. Had she been a bad girl, too bad to put up with?
She still didn't know why her father didn't come to take
her home with him, couldn't understand where her
mother was. This dilemma, she reasoned, could be only
because she was bad. Had Donnie and Stevie discarded
her, too? For certain she'd grow a purple nose now; no
amount of cookies could help her. There was nothing
for her to do as a four- and five-year-old but sit on the
plastic pad of the chrome-legged chair in Aunt Nellie's
kitchen and try to be good for her.

It was Nellie's house, Nellie's table, her pillows, and
her cookies. They weren't Cathy's; never would be hers,
not like a home had once been hers with all its chairs,
bowls, and drawers. And Nellie let Cathy know in no
uncertain terms that she was there only because of
Nellie's own big heart. She would be *good!* She would.
She would learn to be a good girl.

Later that summer, Aunt Nellie started training Cathy
by teaching her small daily tasks which she performed
while Nellie sat nearby and supervised. Cathy learned to
fold the towels (all edges even), water the plants, pour
coffee and tea, set the table, weed the garden, and
balance on a chair at the kitchen sink to suds up and
swish-swash Nellie's white plastic dishes. These activities were like a game to Cathy. "You're becoming a
good little helper," Aunt Nellie acknowledged, and
Cathy carried that spoken prize to bed with her, pleased
with herself for pleasing Aunt Nellie. "I'm a good little
helper, I'm a good little helper."

Nellie's house was filled with collections of things:
old perfume bottles, pencils, coasters, doilies, tobacco
boxes, linens, glassware, knickknacks of every descrip-

tion; on the walls were plaques with inscriptions such as, "May the wind always be at your back" and the Prayer of Saint Francis of Assisi. In the kitchen were odd-matched bowls and glasses, framed photographs of her family perched on the TV set and counter tops, various appliances, junk mail, advertisements, and coupons. There was the apple barrel at the bottom of the base-ment stairs and the mind-boggling assortment of canned jellies, jams, pickles, fruits, and vegetables lining the wall.

Cathy was especially interested in the telephone because she knew her mother's or father's voice might be heard when it rang.

Aunt Nellie's voice couldn't be missed when she talked on the telephone, so Cathy always heard the con-versation. She had a habit of shouting into the receiver as though the wires were powerless on their own. So Cathy would hear conversations with Carol, Nellie's granddaughter. She heard her saying, "Well, she's just a poor little tyke. If I don't keep her, the State will prob-ably come and take her away somewhere. Put her in an orphanage or something. So, as long as the check comes every month. . . ."

Sometimes Aunt Nellie would tell a caller, "I've had so many troubles with other children, like the boys I've had to send back to the State. This little gal is no prob-lem so far. . . ."

And then this conversation with Cathy's father: "Don, I think it would be best if you *didn't* come by to see Cathy tonight. The poor little tyke needs her sleep, and bedtime is half-past seven. Besides, she always gets so upset when you leave. Maybe you'd better not come for a while—until she's really used to it here. . . ."

Cathy came to recognize Nellie's signals: the stiff jerk of her head, the pinched mouth and cocked eye; to these she hastily gave compliance. If she committed an infrac-tion that drew a sterner reprimand than a look from Nellie, such as, "When you wash a cup, be sure you wash it *clean*," she was quick to correct herself. If Nellie had looked with a sensitive eye she would have seen the girl gnawing her fingers in self-reproach and her face puckered in consternation. She wanted to please.

"Cathy, did you leave these tracks on the floor? How many times have I told you to wipe off your feet on the mat before you come traipsing in the kitchen?"

Just that tone of voice made her feel horrible. Two things terrified her, though she couldn't have expressed it at the time: one was the fear of loss, and the second was fear of punishment. She still believed she was the reason for her parents' divorce, and thought Mommy and Daddy had sent her away because she was a bad girl.

4

NELLIE MUST HAVE noticed the child's nervousness because she spoke to Bill about it. "That child is as jumpy as all get-out. I wonder if she'll ever get used to it here?"

"Sure she will. She's still a baby. Give her time."

"But she's always got that hand stuck in her mouth."

"Well, all kids do that, don't they?"

The boy Billy came into the kitchen making his stilted, crooked movements and handed Uncle Bill the evening newspaper. He was a boy too large for his ten years and he stood at the table watching their faces with a half smile. "Billy, thank you for bringing in the paper. Now you can go outside in the backyard and play with Cathy." The boy's face broke into a grin, displaying his mouth full of crooked teeth. Then he went out the back door on legs that barely bent when he moved.

"I don't know what more I can do to make Cathy happy here," Nellie continued. "What if she winds up like Billy?"

"That's ridiculous. She's a normal little girl, Ma. Billy's got brain damage, he's retarded. Cathy is just scared in a new place, that's all."

"I don't feel adequate, Bill" (she emphasized the word *adequate*). "I don't know if I've got the stamina or the gumption anymore."

Bill offered, "I'll help in every way I can. Maybe I should be giving her more attention." He began reading the sports section of the paper and Nellie reached for the financial section.

They were still sitting that way when Cathy opened the kitchen door and carefully wiped her feet on the mat in front of it. She was smiling and excited and when she had Aunt Nellie's eye, she produced from behind her back a tiny fistful of geraniums. She handed them to Nellie as a gift and Nellie, stunned that her geranium heads were nipped off their stems in the flowerpot, took them from her, and was about to admonish, "Don't pick my flowers!" but she saw the bitten baby fingers, and instead thanked her with a hesitant smile.

Did she want more flowers? "No, dear, these will do. The rest should stay in the pot for now." The five-year-old beamed. Would Aunt Nellie say she was a good girl?

"That's a good girl, Cathy. I'll call you when it's time for supper."

"Can I help make supper, Aunt Nellie?"

"Of course you can," and she almost opened her great fleshy arms to embrace the child, but she took a sip of coffee instead. Cathy beamed.

Bill chuckled from behind the newspaper. "And you said you're getting too old to take care of kids."

That evening after supper when the four of them sat in the living room watching TV, Bill caught the eye of the little girl who was perched on the couch across the room nervously picking at her fingers. He winked and patted his lap and she shyly came to him.

She fell asleep there on his lap just before the telephone rang. Bill carried her to her bed with Billy hopping alongside as Nellie asked Mr. Crowell, "How long will you be gone, Don?"

With both children tucked in their beds, Bill stopped to pick up a small patent leather shoe with *Mary Jane* written on the label inside. He smiled, remembering Buster Brown, who used to live in his shoe when he was a boy. But this tiny shoe in his hand no longer fit the child. He surveyed the barren room and made a mental list: first, new shoes; second, new toys.

"Well, good luck to you both," Nellie was saying into the telephone, and then, "Don't you worry about your daughter. She'll be fine until you return. Have a good time and best to your new missus."

Aunt Nellie allowed the hall light to burn through the night so Cathy could see for herself there were no ghosts coming to get her, even though once in a while she still dreamed of ghosts taking her mother away. In her dreams her mother sobbed as she had the last time Cathy saw her. It would be several years before she would see her again.

Morning faithfully arrived and Cathy became part of the motion of Nellie's world. Jelly jars filled with geranium blossoms lined the windowsills in Nellie's kitchen. The morning smell of coffee brewing filled the house and she was a good girl, stirring oatmeal or painting margarine blankets on slices of toast. Beside her on another chair sat Mr. Cuddly Dudley.

Fall arrived and Aunt Nellie's strong will overcame her aches and pains to accept the three-times-daily drive to her job as a crossing guard for elementary-school children. Cathy accompanied her at these appointed times and waited in the car while the seventy-five-year-old woman, poised like a performing bear in the middle of the street, whistled and brandished a SCHOOL-STOP sign in her hand, offering safety to the children skittering from one curb to another. Nellie performed her job with relish. Cathy watched unhappily from the car because she hated just sitting with Cuddly Dudley beside her instead of playing outside. One thing caught her attention and entertained her thoughts for several moments each time she sat waiting. It was the uniforms the children wore. She told Aunt Nellie she liked the uniforms because she thought they were pretty and everybody looked alike. Though she didn't have the right words, she meant they looked like a *family*. Aunt Nellie decided then and there it was time to enroll Cathy in school.

"It looks like her father has up and abandoned her," Nellie sighed to herself.

He hadn't abandoned her! One afternoon when Cathy was standing at the stove next to Aunt Nellie, swirling syrup in a pan for taffy, the old woman told her that her father was coming over. A whoop of delight! She began dancing in circles. She ran to get the new things Aunt Nellie and Uncle Bill had gotten her. She washed her face, put on barrettes. She jumped—no, hopped—to her place under the bed where she kept her new underwear and socks. Billy sat as still as a cat as Cathy flew around the house.

"He's not coming until later," Nellie crowed after her. "You've got plenty of time; not until dinner. Settle down or you'll blow a gasket."

He's coming for me! He's coming for me!

And he came. Cathy saw the shiny new car pull up in front of the house.

"Cathleen, Aunt Nellie is moving to a new house and you'll be able to have your own room there," her father said.

"Can't I go home with you?"

"No, it's better for you with Aunt Nellie. Don't you like Aunt Nellie?"

Aunt Nellie sat plump as a penguin in her chair in her living room, her eye upon the little girl who became flustered and jammed her fingers into her mouth. "I—I—but—"

What Cathy wanted to convince her father of was that she longed to go home with him. She didn't want to stay with Aunt Nellie anymore. She wanted her own daddy and her own family. What she did say was, "Yes, but—"

Her father grinned. "That's my girl. You'll be happier with Aunt Nellie and Uncle Bill. They tell me that you have lots of fun playing outside and being Aunt Nellie's helper. Aunt Nellie will take good care of you, you'll see."

Please take me home, she whispered so only she could hear it. *I want to go home with you. Please, please take me home.*

Aunt Nellie got her check and then he was gone, pleased with himself. Cathy had watched them as they spoke in muffled tones, frantically seeking comfort from the fingers in her mouth. Yes, yes, her father knew Nellie would take good care of Cathy—yes, she was a nice little girl to have around, no problem—her mother simply couldn't handle the girl plus the boys, and he, well, Pat and he . . .

"Sure, Don, don't worry about a thing. Cathy's fine. . . ." He was relieved that his daughter was well cared for and he could leave with a calm mind. After Nellie moved and was settled in her new place, she'd see about taking the boys.

Neither adult observed the child raking miserably at the bodice of her new dress with her fingers, fretting at what was taking place. When she could hold it no longer, she burst into a long, high wail which continued for several minutes, even after the gleaming new car had vanished around the corner on its way to the freeway.

5

Autumn 1967

NELLIE ENROLLED THE girl in school; it seemed only right; if she didn't take the bull by the horns and do something for this child, who would?

She explained to Cathy that all children had to go to school. But Cathy didn't want to go away. Billy didn't have to go to school, and he cried because he didn't want to be left out.

Nellie bought Cathy some brown penny loafers to wear to school. Cathy clung to Nellie's legs; she screamed with panic when Nellie dropped her off at the monster school to start first grade. Nellie comforted herself with talk of doing her duty; after all, the girl would get used to it soon. Just give her time. But it was being *left* that terrified Cathy; being cut off, being an extension of nothing. Her fear was so great that she would later have no memory of the classroom, who the other children were, or what she did there.

Nellie had decided it was time to move. She bought a home in Beverly Hills. For months there were towering stacks of boxes and overstuffed paper bags piled in corners and along the walls. Rooms of furniture in rows formed thick, high banks throughout the house, between which were little rivers of floor to pass along. Cathy didn't recognize the house anymore. She

searched for familiar objects and rescued old toys from
a paper bag along with some magazines to be thrown
out. She put them back beside her frayed Cuddly
Dudley on her bed.

Billy seemed more and more agitated as these changes
took place. He sulked and burst into rages easily. He
couldn't communicate his fears and resented Cathy
because she had become one of "them," those in the
other world where he wasn't allowed. "I want to go to
school," he cried. He didn't want to play anymore. He
stomped and sulked and sang odd little songs that
sounded like advertisements from TV. When he started
to play with matches and lit a fire one day, Cathy cow-
ered behind a column of boxes, barely breathing, waiting for what Aunt Nellie might do to him. She had seen
her brothers punished when they were naughty and it
frightened her. Spankings were terrible. She had only
been spanked once, when she wet the bed at her father's
place in Chicago. To be punished means you're bad, but
her brothers couldn't be bad because they loved her. It
was okay if Billy got punished because Billy didn't love
her.

Aunt Nellie didn't scream or yell and Billy did not get
spanked. He was told he couldn't play outside for a
week and made to sit in the corner until supper. The fire
itself was a fascination, a triumph of golden angry
flames. Billy had stood back and observed his creation
with pride, and Cathy had watched, amazed at the
magic he had performed. *"Boys!"* Nellie sighed, shaking her cheeks.

"I don't want him going back to the State," Aunt Nellie
complained to Uncle Bill. "They'll treat him like the
other kids, like he isn't different. I'm telling you that
boy's retarded, and the other kids will hurt him. That's
why I've kept him home, so he wouldn't be hurt.

"You'd think the State would have the sense to let
him be where he's cared for good."

"But what if he starts another fire—a serious one?"

4

They finally agreed that Billy would have to go back.

"Just don't let them tell you sending him back is *my* fault. It's not *my* fault he's touched in the head. I certainly did the best I could."

And if they'd send Billy away to the State when he wasn't bad enough to spank, what would they do to her if she was bad?

Chicago, Illinois
1968

The move wasn't easy on Nellie Landers. After all, she was seventy-seven years old now. The house she bought was an old, narrow, white wood frame house with a wood-railed porch and green shutters on the windows. Low box hedges framed the short walkway from the front yard and led up the steps from the sidewalk. On either side were spots of thin, faded grass. ("We'll have to do something about this lawn right away, Bill. Don't forget.") The house was in Beverly Hills, the nation's largest urban historic district (as registered in the *National Register of Historic Places*, 1981), a neighborhood sitting atop Blue Island Ridge, the highest land in Cook County.

Cathy followed Aunt Nellie and Uncle Bill up the walk, pondering the notion of *her* room; they had said she'd have her *own* room. And she did, too: a converted den off the living room, just for her.

The house became not just Aunt Nellie's, but Aunt Nellie herself, just as the other house had been. Her presence was in every room, filling it wall to wall with Nellie Landers' smells and sounds, doilies, photographs in tarnished frames, scatter rugs and unmatched end tables; her rolling, slow movement, her TV programs, and the floating scent of camphor. The furniture was put in place and the knickknacks placed on the shelves.

They kept living with Nellie's things, just as they had before.

Cathy's room was small, with one window above the bed. In the corner stood a brown metal wardrobe for a closet. A wooden dresser stood on the other wall, and a flowered curtain hung across the door frame.

Aunt Nellie and Uncle Bill didn't talk about much except matters concerning the house, the chores that needed to be done, and expenses. Then came the angry complaints, which Cathy imagined centered around her. But in spite of the double message of caring and complaining, she began to feel more at ease with Aunt Nellie and Uncle Bill. Her shyness with them was gone. She waited for Uncle Bill's smiling invitation to climb on his lap and begged for more when he tickled, wrestled, or played tag around the living room with her.

Uncle Bill returned home each night from work as a maintenance engineer for the city schools with a surprise for a happy, squealing little girl. She waited for him on the porch, straining to see his figure appear at the corner. Then her whole body became buoyant and she jumped from the porch with legs pedaling the air to run and meet him.

At the supper table Aunt Nellie had complaints she couldn't hide. It didn't matter that the little girl sat between them. Nellie would rave about the injustices of life, particularly when it pertained to foster parenting.

"I always say people who don't like kids shouldn't go around having them." Bill, who was neither married nor a parent, looked up and started to add an important thought of his own, but decided against it as Nellie continued: "Here they go and have those three kids and now they don't know what to do with them. Well, I blame the mother."

Bill tore a slice of bread in half and drenched it in the chicken gravy on his plate. He wiped his mouth with a paper napkin and reached for the little girl who sat quietly staring at her plate. She scrambled from her chair and climbed onto his lap. "Aw, you used to like kids, Ma . . . you must be getting old," was what he wanted to say, but Nellie passed him some more creamed corn.

"You're not finished already? Most people who take in kids are probably still looking for their own. Maybe they went away—maybe they died—but nobody else's kid is ever really your own. You're always the baby-sitter." She said this as though warning him. "I read about a man and woman who have forty foster children living with them right now. All of them are crippled or retarded. I don't know how they do it. Cathy, get your fingers out of your mouth. It's a crazy world to bring kids into—especially girls. A boy can protect himself—at least that's what I always used to think. Here it is 1968 and you see the world and the way it is now, with Vietnam and the riots we're having in this country. It makes you wonder. And look at the immorality. Just look at it. Girls are running around in clothes they used to only show in girlie houses. It wasn't this way when you were young, Bill, I'll tell you that. Sometimes I wonder why people go on having kids at all . . . and you shouldn't get too attached, either, Bill."

6

Summer and Autumn 1968

CATHY COULD TELL there was something wrong. She knew Nellie's clues. She could tell without a word when Nellie Landers was upset, nervous, sick, or angry.

Upset: she knew Nellie was upset when the things she handled were heavier and when her feet were heavier, too. Aunt Nellie thumped and banged the lightest objects as though they were blocks of stone, and she stomped the floor as though she were killing bugs with every step.

Nervous: Nellie would sit with her arms crossed in front of her, impatiently clicking her teeth and drumming her fingers on any surface. One eye glowered. Her voice was higher than usual.

Sick: When Aunt Nellie was sick she didn't need to say a word, for just by seeing the forlorn, childlike expression on her face, her helpless sighing, and her slouched posture, Cathy was at her side waiting for instructions to bring her some aid in hopes of making her feel good again.

Angry: This was what Cathy feared most of all, because it was at those times Aunt Nellie sealed her lips and her whole huge presence became a silent, vacant lot.

Today Nellie was nervous. She sat cross-armed at the table, clicking her teeth while examining a list of expenses for the month. Cathy hurried from the kitchen after breakfast to go out into the backyard, away from Nellie's mood. She spent most of the morning lying in the grass beneath the branches of the oak tree growing over the cinnamon pointed roof of the house. The leaves fluttered, blinked, like opening and closing eyes above her head, and she imagined the whole world twitched and crossed its arms at her. Then her eyes grew heavy and she fell asleep.

Cathy vaguely heard the taxi pull up in front of the house, but the grass held her captive and she didn't stir. There were voices, doors opening and closing, and the high call of Aunt Nellie floating over it all. Then the screen door of the kitchen clapped open, flew wide, slapped tight again, and her brothers, Donnie and Stevie, were skipping across the yard. She heard Nellie's cracked voice from the window: "Don't slam the door!" Then, "Is that Cathy in the grass over there? She's going to get eaten alive! Bring her inside. Watch out or you'll step on those agapanthus—they're not weeds!" Nellie watched from the window with eyes narrowed as the boys approached the sleeping form.

"Hey, Squirt! Get that mosquito on her cheek."

"Hey! Wake up."

She awoke to the sting on her face and looked into the faces of two older, larger, strange boys. It frightened her at first and then shyly she scratched the itch on her cheek and arms and sat up to face them.

"Well, whattaya know, Squirt? You've gotten bigger!"

But she didn't know them and she turned toward the safety of the house where Aunt Nellie stood with her arms crossed, clicking her teeth and watching from the window.

They ambled and played, teased and sauntered through the next short weeks with the abandon of children. Cathy was happy again. It wasn't long before she returned to being their sister again. But she wasn't the new, older child: she became the four-year-old who had

left them. She whined, cried, even squawked, when she
wanted her own way. Again she was the "spoiled brat,"
as they used to call her. Aunt Nellie tolerated this
behavior with clicking, tapping impatience, until stomp-
ing out her indignation, she proclaimed there would be
no more of that or she would send them all away.

They had refuge in each other, frowning at rebukes
and giggling at the power they had to disobey. "Will
you stay here forever?" she asked them.

"Naw. Probably go back to Mom's—who knows?"

"We've been sort of everywhere, Squirt. School,
Mom's, on our own, you name it."

"*Mom*. Where's Mommy?"

"She'll be here, don't you worry."

Donnie tried to teach the little girl to print her name,
but she couldn't concentrate. *Mommy!* "It's like this,
see, a half circle, that's C. Now you do it—you're old
enough to be able to write your name, you know. Come
on, now make the tent, see, up and down with a bar
across, that's *A*—no, not a *X*, that's not—don't you
like your name? Let's try again." Her fingers were like
jelly holding the pencil in her hand. The urging of Donnie's voice made her anxious. Anxiety blocked out her
ability to follow what he was saying because she clicked
off, went blank. Days later, under the tree in the yard,
she spelled out O-R-A-N-G-E for him and he told
Stevie, "See there? She's not so dumb. She can spell
orange. That's not exactly easy."

They climbed the cherry trees in the neighbor's yard
and threw down cherries for Cathy to eat. They ran,
played, brought other boys around the house, and it
became, for a while, "their" house, and Cathy was part
of it.

"How come you don't know how to tie your shoes,
Squirt? Come on, I'll show you. You can't go to the
new school without knowing how to tie your shoes, you
know."

"Are you going to the new school, too, Stevie?" He
didn't answer.

She whined and clung to them; she continued to obey

Aunt Nellie but didn't jump to please her. She wanted
to be with her brothers. If they were gone, she waited
anxiously; if they were busy with other things, she in-
truded, nagged, and pouted for their attention. The
temper tantrums were the last straw.

Nellie got on the telephone with their father: "It's not
good for her, I'm telling you, Don, it's just not good.
You'll have to come up with something. Not that I don't
care for them all, each of them, and I've always pre-
ferred boys—but it's a bad influence!"

Stevie told Cathy she'd like the new school in the new
neighborhood; school was a place to have fun and play
with other kids, learn things, too, even how to print
her name, *Cathleen*, correctly, and no, silly, he said, it
wasn't like the State, she must have it mixed up in her
head or something. Besides, he wondered, how come
she was so worried and scared about the State anyhow?

Well, she *was* worried. She recognized Aunt Nellie's
nonverbal signals: the flashing eyes, the tight, pinched
lips, the silences. And Nellie was eating more jam and
jellies, topping her nightly ice cream with gobs of it, and
she knew better. Uncle Bill was quieter, too. A thought-
ful face took the place of his other, happier one. In the
evening after work he went directly for the newspaper
without a hello from the little girl who used to wait for
him.

Then school started. Aunt Nellie marched Cathy up
the walk leading to the long, low, red brick buildings
past the white gleaming statue of Saint Barnabas. Cathy
wasn't as terrified this time at the swirling forms of
children around her. It wasn't like that first school
where she had evaporated within its walls. These children, amid the towering forms of nuns, were each and
every one of them dressed exactly like her.

But one day when Cathy returned from school her
brothers were nowhere to be found. No one told her
where they went or who took them. And when she cried,
Aunt Nellie reminded her of her nice uniform and all the
new friends she'd make at school. Her loneliness for her
brothers remained like a sore that kept opening.

Nellie's great-grandchildren, David and Mark Smith,
often came to visit. They were close to Cathy's age.
Nellie had a special affection for them because they
were her own blood, and their presence made the house
seem much different from when Cathy's brothers were
there. Mark and David's mother was Carol Smith, Aunt
Nellie's granddaughter. She was an energetic, outgoing
lady, and very grateful to Aunt Nellie. Aunt Nellie was
good to Carol, and she loved her, anyone could tell.
Nellie always assured Carol that things would be okay;
she'd help out. Cathy had never heard her talk that way.
Her words of encouragement were because of Bernie
Smith, Carol's handsome, strong husband, who had
had an accident. He had fallen twenty-five feet from a
blast burner at Inland Steel and shattered his spine. The
tragedy struck cruelly because it left him a paraplegic
confined to a wheelchair. When it happened, Carol was
eight months pregnant with her second son, David. The
one who had helped her most through these dark hours
was her grandmother, Aunt Nellie.

Bernie's long and painful recovery in the hospital
could have devastated them financially, but Aunt Nellie
stepped in and helped pay the bills. She was loyal to her
family. Carol proved to be of the same strong fabric as
her grandmother; she was determined not to allow the
accident to derail their lives. She went to work after the
baby was born and kept the family's spirits up by sheer
determination, which she'd learned from Nellie. These
two strong women were Cathy's primary female role
models. They contrasted with the memories of her
mother, who seemed powerless.

The last time Cathy saw her mother was in a hospital
cafeteria, where she was picking at her food. Her
cigarette was burning in the ashtray. She spoke in short
little nervous gasps. When her father took Cathy away
that afternoon, screaming and kicking, her mother only
watched helplessly with vacant, confused eyes. She
seemed so tiny in that gray place, so small and defense-
less. Carol and Aunt Nellie were not like that. The

world didn't swallow them. Cathy didn't know if she belonged to any of them.

When Cathy went off to school, Nellie became more protective. She did allow Cathy to walk to school each day with her new friend, Liz, who came from a happy, rowdy family of six children. Each day when Liz went home to a noisy lunch of sandwiches in her kitchen, Cathy ate alone in the car while Nellie guarded her crossing site. Cathy still wanted to please her, and if it helped, she lied to avoid Nellie's piercing, angry eyes.

"Why are you late?"

"I was kept after school to help Sister."

"What did you help her do?"

"Oh, stack up papers, things like that. She likes me." (*I was playing with Liz down the street, Aunt Nellie, but you would be very angry if you knew that.*)

At home Cathy could now wash and dry dishes without the aid of a chair to stand on; she could dust, make beds, and vacuum the floors. Nellie taught her how to run the washing machine and she washed clothes and folded them while Nellie watched from her chair in the kitchen. Nellie was in pain most of the time now, and her vision was becoming clouded with cataracts. But her will was still strong.

The old woman hated what was happening to her body. It had become her enemy, interfering with the pursuits of her mind. She owned real estate, pored over papers and contracts daily, and kept a steady grip on what was hers. And that included the little girl. The child was growing up and before she knew it, she'd be developing physically. She'd have to be watched, controlled. Disciplined. Oh, girls were so much more work than boys. It wouldn't be easy.

Duty, that's what it was. Responsibility. If you could have seen that child on her seventh birthday, sick as a dog, with those infected tonsils of hers. Who was it who took her over to the hospital and had those tonsils taken out? Nellie, that's who. Her father off in Portugal somewhere, even though he was a nice enough man and he had his own worries, what with his heart attack and all, but who did that leave to take care of his girl? Nellie, that's who. Nellie watched over the poor thing, visited her in the hospital, brought her home, fed her ice cream, but who did she ask for when she came out of the anesthesia? And who did she cry for at night? Her *mother*. A woman she hadn't seen since she was a baby.

The divorce papers said that Cathy's mother, Georgia Crowell, had custody of the three children and that Don, the father, was to pay their support. There was only one thing Nellie couldn't understand about that divorce. It was granted on the grounds of cruelty. Donald Crowell didn't seem cruel to Nellie Landers. So the mother got custody.

Maybe Nellie ought to think about doing something about that. She'd better be cautious. After all, that woman wanted her little girl back. Nellie had her contacts and their telephone calls were a sore reminder that Georgia was working a job, saving her money, and living for the day when she could have her children with her again. And Cathy, who knew nothing, not one pinprick of her family's whereabouts, could only dream and do her best to please Aunt Nellie.

7

1969

THE WORLD SEEMED to stretch and expand when Cathy was eight years old. She discovered there was more beyond the doors than the walk to Saint Barnabas School. What was more, she learned that she wouldn't disintegrate to dust, or be swallowed by a crack in the earth, if she went exploring the community. She also didn't become *lost* as Nellie had warned she would. (*Lost*, along with similar words such as *death, kill, the State, abandoned, alone,* and *unwanted*, evoked great anxiety in Cathy. Nellie seemed to know exactly when to use these words.)

Cathy discovered curving streets that wound through old neighborhoods of squat brick houses, like the one Liz lived in with her slew of brothers and sisters, and neighborhoods that were dotted with tiny parks which popped up like surprise candy. She'd stop to swing or slide there, or lie in the grass and pretend things she couldn't remember later. Some of the streets she wandered along looped back upon themselves, but always curving, meandering, and presenting some new discovery. And she did make discoveries, like the mansions that perched on the top of the ridge peering out at the countryside below, and the old nineteenth-century houses with their pale gray shutters and wrought-iron balconies, sitting on enormous lots, like green fields, on Prospect Avenue overlooking Graver Park. It was there Cathy and Liz went to play after school, though Nellie forbade her to go.

One day Liz met Cathy in the rain on the way to school. She was a year older than Cathy. Some mornings they walked to school behind Liz's brothers, who ignored them. Liz invited Cathy to share her red plastic see-through umbrella, and they sloshed along Wood Street beside the dripping clipped hedges, chattering the way old buddies do. Liz wanted to walk home at lunchtime with Cathy, and at that moment, Cathy felt her first pang of embarrassment and anger at Aunt Nellie. She had to answer that she didn't go home for lunch.

"How come?"

She thought of lying but instead risked, "I meet my aunt and have lunch with her."

"In a restaurant?"

"No . . . in her car. She's a crossing guard. I eat lunch in the car while she crosses the kids. That's how she wants it. She doesn't want me walking home alone unless she's going to be really late."

"Can I come with you sometime?"

Her request surprised Cathy—in fact, to be liked so readily was a surprise. The other kids at school were statues to her, unapproachable and unreal, even though they wore the same uniforms. Liz didn't laugh at Cathy when she told her about Aunt Nellie and that she was a foster child and Aunt Nellie wasn't her real aunt.

Children darted everywhere at Liz's house, where the sounds of radios and television going at the same time didn't seem to bother anyone. Cathy felt a difference there; she didn't feel tension or panic to please. There was a constant disarray of shifting articles: clothing heaped in clumps on the floor, coffee cups stuck to saucers and on the coffee table in the living room, scatter rugs that were rumpled on the floor, and dishes perpetually occupying the sink. Liz's mother was easygoing, not manipulative; she was pliable, even jolly; not like the hard, demanding Nellie. Now Cathy started to feel conscious resentment toward Nellie. Every night before she went to sleep she would fantasize about her mother coming to get her. She prayed to the Virgin Mother, who she believed was perfect and good and understood her as her real mother would. She wanted someone to hug her the way Liz's mother hugged Liz. This image of her mother was all Cathy believed she had.

The other kids at school teased Cathy for not having parents. They laughed at her and called her "Crow" instead of Crowell, cawing at her. The girls in her class laughed at Aunt Nellie and called her names Cathy had never heard of. They pointed at the old woman and made fun of her as she squinted owlishly at them, not knowing they were laughing at her.

Liz was different. She didn't laugh or make fun of her. She had dark hair and eyes like Cathy, and she was tall for her age. After school one day Cathy brought Liz home and fearfully introduced her to Aunt Nellie. "This is Liz O'Connell, my friend from school."

"You're Irish, then?"

"Yes, ma'am." As if that were all in the world necessary to know, Aunt Nellie dismissed her by diverting her attention to Cathy. "Chores to be done before playing, young lady."

She reassessed her rules, tightened them, made new restrictions, drawing Cathy closer, tighter. "Chores to be done," "Can't go out of the yard," "Be home immediately after school," "Stay where I can see you," "You can't be out after dark," "No staying late on the playground," "No riding your bike up the hill," "Spit that gum out, you'll get cavities and who will pay for the dentist?" "You're lucky I took you in. Where would you be if I hadn't?" "You can't go to the movies, not even with Liz's mother, movies are nothing but filth and trash—"

Filth and trash. Cathy began to be aware that Nellie's assessment of the world outside her domain was filth and trash. But Cathy wondered if that was what she was. In a vague, dreamy sort of way, she suspected she might be of that world Nellie feared.

In 1969 Nellie Landers was seventy-eight years old, and the world around her seemed to be shrinking. Days were shorter; the details of everyday life somehow took on intense importance. Things like putting the jar lid back on the jam, how the orange juice container was placed in the refrigerator, eating what she wanted to, and making sure everybody was in her sight and where they ought to be. Cathy didn't like Nellie closing in around her like an angry vise; it gave her such bad feelings.

In the mornings Nellie and Cathy piled in the old Ambassador and Nellie drove to the church for early mass. Cathy was certain Nellie dropped her off so early to get rid of her, but it didn't matter after a while. She had questions about God. She was fascinated with the idea of heaven and knowing God. One morning as she sat in the church all alone, she wondered how she could ever be good enough to get to heaven. As soon as she walked out of the church she would be bad again. It troubled her. She thought of God watching her and pointing a finger at her to remind her of how bad she was. How could she do penance for all that was wrong with her? It was confusing. She sighed and guessed only nuns and priests were perfect.

When she was seven she had made her First Communion. It was a big event for her because for once she was the focus of attention. For a child who wanted so badly to be accepted and seemed to be getting nowhere at it, it was a special day. Aunt Nellie took her shopping for a dress, and she felt important and grown-up. After Aunt Nellie picked out the right dress for her—white with netting and little polyester roses—Cathy chose her veil. She came right out and said what she wanted, which was unusual for her; she usually didn't communicate what her real wants were anymore because too often they weren't realized. This time, because she felt important and happy, she surprised herself and spoke up. But Nellie said, "No, you won't look good in that veil," and bought her a different kind instead.

Uncle Bill, Aunt Nellie, Carol, and Bernie came to the First Communion service, and someone else came to make the event even more special: her father.

That was the year she decided she was going to be a nun. That way she'd be perfect.

8

NELLIE'S PUNISHMENTS GREW more frequent each year. When Cathy did something Nellie didn't like, Nellie grounded her. That meant she couldn't play outside after school or in the evening or on Saturday or at any time. It meant staying confined in the house with the smells of camphor and cleaning powders, the heat up too high, stuffy and dark. If she lied with enough skill and Liz's help, the punishments wouldn't be so bad.

"Do you know what you're going to tell your Aunt Nellie this time? Have you got it figured out?"

"Well, I'll just tell her I'm late because I couldn't help it."

"That's a terrible excuse. You won't be able to go out for a week. I'll never see you. You'll get locked up and she'll throw away the key!"

"Well, how's this, then—Aunt Nellie, I was on my way home from school and I realized I had left my library book on the lawn at school. So I had to go back and get it. Liz came with me. We went back to get my book, but it wasn't there."

Liz approved. "So far, so good."

"So we went inside and Sister Agnes saw us and asked us where we were going, so I told her and she said—"

Liz took over, ". . . she said we could look in the Lost

and Found, so we walked to the office to find the Lost and Found, but the lady was gone for the day. Then we tried to leave, but the back door was locked, so we had to walk all around the front to get out. It must have taken at least ten more minutes—''

"Liz, Aunt Nellie doesn't like long stories."

"Well, tell her you have to explain all of it so she'll really believe you."

"Okay, so then I'll tell her that we were leaving school and we saw your brother. We told him I lost my library book, and he told us maybe it was at your house because one of your other brothers might have found it and brought it home, knowing it was mine."

"She might not like that. She doesn't like you being around boys, does she?"

"Oh, I forgot. Okay, so it was your sister who found the book. So then we go over to your house, and we look for my book, and we can't find it, right?"

When Cathy got to this part of her story with Aunt Nellie later, Nellie said, "I've heard enough." Cathy looked at her with the most innocent face she could muster and said, "It's the *truth*, Aunt Nellie, *honest*."

The real truth was, she had been playing kickball a block away. Elaborate lies, she found, sounded more truthful.

Most of the time her stories succeeded; sometimes she was clumsy and got caught. Once when she was grounded (unfairly in her opinion), she drew an ugly face with chalk on the patio in the backyard. She drew a long, pointed nose and big eyes like tennis balls, and horns growing out of the head. Beneath it she printed, NELLIE LANDERS THE WITCH. Later Uncle Bill spotted it and said quietly as he passed her on his way to the porch, "You'd better wash off the patio." She panicked.

"Why?" (Trying to sound innocent.)

"Don't you know why?"

"What's wrong with the patio?" (Blank expression on her face.)

"Go on out and see for yourself," he said casually, not threateningly.

She had to defend herself. "Oh! Now I think I understand what you're talking about. *I* didn't draw that picture. Connie Martin did. You see, she was mad because Aunt Nellie hollered at her today."

Uncle Bill simply shrugged and repeated, "I think you'd better wash that sidewalk with the hose pretty quick."

The words rushed from her mouth: "Connie Martin was real mad, Uncle Bill. I wasn't even there. I've been inside most of the day. *Honest. I* didn't do it."

"Don't just stand there yapping, wash it off before Aunt Nellie sees it."

Too late. Aunt Nellie was going out the back door at that very moment. When she came back inside, Cathy met her with a rush of excuses: "Connie Martin did it. I didn't do it; I would never do such a thing, not in your own backyard, Aunt Nellie. Imagine her nerve. She said you hollered at her, which I bet isn't even true. Of course, I only just heard about it because I was in the house all day long. I was cleaning the bathroom, just like you told me to. I also straightened up your papers in your room."

But she didn't tell Aunt Nellie about the newspaper clipping she found—the one with the photo of Pat, her father's wife, standing in front of their room divider of semiprecious stones. She didn't tell Aunt Nellie that she knew where her father lived now. The article said they lived at Lake Point Towers in Chicago.

Aunt Nellie forbade her to play with Connie Martin ever again. She also was never to play with any of Connie's brothers. The lesson Cathy learned was this: Be careful who you blame for things. Because if you are forbidden to play with someone and you do, you have to concoct more stories—like the tales she had to tell Nellie whenever she played with Connie Martin and her brothers after that.

Cathy was convinced Nellie didn't like children. She

had to lie to go to Liz's house. "I went to the store, Aunt Nellie. Honest."

"It doesn't take two hours to go to the store."

"Well, just when I was almost home, I discovered I bought the wrong thing and I had to go back—not once, but twice."

"No wonder. You'd forget your head if it wasn't—"

"And then I saw that girl named Marcie, you know, the little girl I told you about who had that horrible blood disease? Remember how I had to help her get into the ambulance that time they took her to the hospital?"

"I thought she had a broken leg."

"Oh, yes, that too. But that was another time. Anyhow, I saw her all alone, waiting at the corner to go across the street. I just knew *you* would never let her cross the street alone. So I walked her home, right to the door, and then her mother invited me in for a piece of pie. I told her I couldn't because I had to get home, but she practically dragged me in and so then after having a piece of pie (not as good as the ones you used to make) I came straight home, except for when I dropped my change and had to go look for it."

"I've heard enough. What's that little girl's name again? I'm going to call her mother and see if you were really there."

"Go ahead and call her. But I think they left for the hospital now. You could try her tomorrow, though."

She had tried her hardest to be the perfect girl for Nellie, but it was hard, too hard, and she almost never felt her approval. She thought about her father at the beautiful Lake Point Towers. And she waited for an all-perfect, loving mother who would take her away from Nellie's house.

Cathy kept remembering the first time her mother had come to see her at Aunt Nellie's house in Beverly. Cathy was about seven years old. Her mother stood in the doorway, looking small and frail. Aunt Nellie was like a moose next to her. Her mother wanted to hug her because she bent to reach for her, but Nellie stepped between them and ordered her mother to sit on Bill's brown chair and Cathy to sit on the straight-backed chair across the room by the wall. Then Nellie plunked herself down on the sofa to watch them have their time together. She didn't leave them alone for one minute.

Her mother looked tired but pretty. Her skin was pale and she had bright-red rouge on her cheeks. She sat in the chair nervously twisting her hands, and Cathy did the same in the chair across the room. It would have embarrassed Cathy if her mother had actually succeeded in hugging her because she no longer really knew her. (She felt bad when she thought about it later. She really wanted to be hugged, but not right then. Did that make her mother feel bad? Would her mother come back to see her if she didn't hug?) Cathy wasn't accustomed to hugging because Nellie never did. She thought Nellie didn't like anyone touching her. Cathy never learned to express affection, or to say, "I love you." She sat staring at the stranger who was her mother, thinking so many confusing thoughts. Finally the woman spoke: "Cathy, honey, do you like school?"

"Yes, it's okay." (*She's beautiful, an angel.*)

"Are the nuns nice to you?"

"Yes, I guess so." (*She likes me.*)

"What's your favorite subject?"

"I don't know. . . ." (Shrugging, looking at fingernails, fidgeting.) "I suppose I like lots of things. I don't like math, though."

(Smiling.) "You don't? Neither did I when I was your age."

(Shrugging, fidgeting. *I just know she'll take me home with her.*)

"I used to like history. Do you like history, Cathy?"

"Oh, yes." (*Please take me home with you.*)

The mother and daughter glanced anxiously at Aunt Nellie, who was glaring at them. Cathy could tell she was upset because her face was cherry red, as if she were holding her breath. And she was clicking her teeth.

"I'll bet you like to play jump rope, don't you?"

"Oh, sure! I love to jump rope." (*I never jump rope, but I'll say anything to please you.*)

"And I'll bet you're very good at it, too, aren't you?"

"Oh, yes!"

Cathy might not have lied if Aunt Nellie hadn't been there. She wanted to tell her mother how the girls laughed at her when she missed at jump rope. She just knew she would understand. If she could only have told her mother how the kids teased her at school because she didn't have a mother or a father, her mother would have taken her by the hand and told her: "Yes, you do have a mother, Cathy. And I'm here now—your *mother*. You can show the kids they're wrong." She wasn't an orphan, or abandoned, or any of the nasty things they said. This was her mother, her beautiful mother, and she was right there in that very room with her at that very minute.

But then, it seemed so soon, Nellie was saying their goodbyes for them, getting rid of her mother, ushering her out the door. "That's enough, you'll have to go," she said, and Cathy saw the reason was that her mother had started to cry. She gave the most pathetic, hungry look and stretched her arms to her daughter, but she had been warned not to hug the child. Cathy felt something inside her leap forward; she wanted to run into her mother's arms, to be crushed, suffocated in the closeness of her. The longing was so real it made her sob desperately.

Aunt Nellie was really mad. "You've upset her!" The stranger who was her mother left.

Cathy cried for hours, until she finally forced herself to stop. She pleaded with Aunt Nellie: "When is she coming back? *Please* tell me, when will she come back?"

No answers. There were never any answers.

Uncle Bill did his best to make things nicer for her. He bought her first bicycle, and he bought her every bicycle she ever owned after that. He brought home

presents and toys. He gave her what he thought a real
father would give a real daughter. And Cathy began to
regard him as a father. Aunt Nellie often was angry at
him, and he would tell Cathy, "Well, it looks like I'm in
the doghouse again." It became their private little joke
to see who would be in the doghouse the most.

She should have been proud of all the Barbie dolls,
toys, and stuffed animals she owned, but when Liz
looked at all her things and said, "You really are
lucky," Cathy didn't feel lucky or proud. She would
have traded places with Liz because she had what Cathy
really wanted.

It was wintertime and the house was overheated (because Aunt Nellie's bones got cold). The six o'clock
news was just going on when the telephone rang. Cathy
answered it in the front hall, never expecting to hear
what she heard.

"Cathy? Is that you, Squirt?" When she realized it
was the voice of her brother Donnie, she jumped up and
down. Suddenly Uncle Bill's hand clamped over hers,
and he took the receiver away from her. Aunt Nellie
began yelling from the other room. Uncle Bill was saying something into the phone that sounded like, "You
shouldn't be calling here—" Before Cathy could get the
receiver back, he had hung it up and the girl stared in-
credulously at him; she had thought he was her friend.

"Why didn't you let me talk to my brother? That was
my brother Donnie! Why didn't you let me talk to
him?"

Bill lowered his head.

Aunt Nellie was furious. After Cathy was in her bed,
she could still hear the two of them arguing and complaining about her brothers, something about their bad
influence and how it was all her mother's fault.

At Christmastime her brothers braved a visit to her.
Nellie's artificial tree was up, and the manger with the
baby Jesus was sitting on the coffee table along with
the little silver bells and plastic wreaths. Cathy heard the

doorbell and saw her brothers standing on the porch with packages in their arms. She knew they were her brothers even though they looked like grown-ups now. She screamed with delight. But Uncle Bill jumped up, rushed to the door, and told them to leave.

"But can't she at least have her Christmas presents?"

"No, take them with you. She doesn't need them."

The commotion that followed confused the girl; the event remained a mystery to her. She saw their faces in the window. They were knocking and pounding on the glass. Their faces looked smeared with snow, unreal, like drawings that had been half-erased. Cathy was crying and calling their names, and Aunt Nellie yelled something to Uncle Bill about calling the police. That was the last time she saw her brothers for many years.

Aunt Nellie didn't seem to mind as much if her father came to see her, but in the nine years she lived with Nellie, Cathy could have counted the number of his visits on her two hands. Sometimes he took her to Evergreen Plaza to walk around the mall. She was careful not to ask him anymore to take her home with him because she didn't want to make him angry. She was afraid he wouldn't come back again. He seemed especially interested to hear about the vacations Cathy took in Michigan with Aunt Nellie, Uncle Bill, and Nellie's family. Aunt Nellie owned a little cottage near the small town of Mendon. In the summers, and sometimes the winters, too, they drove to the cottage for a day, a week, or more. Her father was pleased to think his little girl was having such a good time.

Actually, the times they went to the little cottage were the happiest times Cathy could remember of her childhood. In the summertime she swam in a lake near Mendon and played with the children who rented the cabins close by. Once Aunt Nellie allowed her to bring a friend with her for a week. Before Aunt Nellie's health started to go, she would can vegetables and fruit, as well as jams and jellies. She did most of the canning at the cottage, and then took it back to Beverly. When Nellie's grandsons Mark and David came to visit, Aunt Nellie took snapshots of the children all together. In these pictures Mark and David were posing happily, with Cathy beside them, except Cathy didn't get in the frame. "Aunt Nellie always manages to cut me off," she said to herself after the pictures were developed.

Nellie wasn't as threatened by the world when she was at the cottage in Michigan. Cathy would simply tell her, "I'm going outside," and that would satisfy her. "Stay where I can see you," was the only thing she demanded.

9

1970

CATHY WAS NINE years old when Nellie drove her in the blue Ambassador to the Chicago Loop to see the lawyer. She didn't talk on the way, just sat in the corner of the front seat by the window, staring out at the Chicago skyline and wishing the sky would fall in. She watched as they passed by rows of old wooden houses with pointed roofs and filmy windows, houses that had been there long before she was born, houses with real families in them, with real parents, where real children played games on living-room floors and jumped on overstuffed furniture, and weren't on the way to a lawyer, where legal custody would be given to a lady called Aunt Nellie.

They took an elevator that smelled like leaky pipes and then they were in the lawyer's library. It was brown, dark, with rows of dusty, ancient books lined up on shelves like forgotten toys. Cathy waited by a window there while Aunt Nellie and the lawyer went to another office to hunch over papers at a desk and talk.

It was the first time in her life Cathy felt there was no hope, no escape, no help. She felt it and couldn't say it, even to herself, but she saw the street below with its swirling, moving shapes and it said to her, "This is the end, Cathy, the end."

So she looked for the lock on the window. She'd have to hurry before Nellie and the lawyer came back to tell her of her fate. Hurry, join the rushing cars below, the pavement where the roots of concrete buildings grew. She couldn't find the lock, couldn't find a way to open the window. She pushed herself against the glass, ran her palms along it. She was imprisoned in that room. She pushed again, pounded—and then she heard the lawyer say, "Shall we begin?"

"I want my mother to have custody of me, not Nellie Landers. I want my real mother and my real father—I want my Cuddly Dudley. I don't want to live with this lady, please! *Call my real mother!*" was what she wanted to say, but instead she said what she thought she was supposed to say.

"Yes, I want to live with Nellie Landers" and "Yes, I'm happy there," while Nellie, trying to read the paper in her hand, didn't look up as she said it.

They drove on Lake Shore Drive and Cathy, spotting the right building, leaned from the car window to debate which window was her father's. Now she belonged to Nellie Landers, who had a paper to prove it. She was a ward of the State in Nellie's custody.

Nellie turned a corner. A truck stalled ahead.

"Star sapphires," Cathy said aloud.

"What's that?" Nellie asked, tooting her horn at the truck.

She was with her father and on his finger was a star sapphire ring. "Oh, Daddy, make your ring sparkle for me!" and he turned his hand and twisted it so the stone cast stars in every direction. "Make the sun shine on it!" and he would, lifting his fingers high in the air so the stars danced. She had loved to hold his hand and watch his star sapphire, dazzling, sparkling, shining. But his hand with the ring sparkling in the sun was somewhere else.

1971

Cathy was ten years old when she started smoking
cigarettes and everybody in the whole neighborhood
knew she smoked because they saw her in the alley or in
their backyards, but if Nellie sniffed as she walked by
and asked her, "Is that smoke I smell?" she said, "Of
course not." She lied about anything, even if she didn't
have to. About baby-sitting ("I'm taking care of the
Evers kid tonight"; she wasn't), about school ("I'm
staying late for Sister"; she wasn't), about swimming in
the lake at Mendon ("I never go deep"; she did), and
about boys ("I don't like boys"; she adored them).

Aunt Nellie hated boys, except her grandsons—at
least that's what Cathy thought. She was ten years old
when she discovered certain secret ways to get all the attention she wanted from boys. By twelve she was even
more experienced. Nellie, who was so mortified of
anyone invading the privacy of her affections and her
body by so much as a hug good night, would have died
on the spot if she knew the parts of her body Cathy was
lending to a neighbor boy for furtive secret times in his
garage. She thought it was revenge, but actually it was
the closest she'd been to tender touching since she was
four years old. And Cathy didn't know about true loving closeness, since she had no memory of it. It amazed
her that it was so easy to get affection, especially as her
body was developing quickly.

PART II

July 1985

It's my second trip to New Hampshire. I'm here to start writing in earnest. David, Cathy's husband, meets me at the baggage pickup at the airport in Boston and we drive up to New Hampshire in his van. He's likable, outgoing, warm. He's open about himself and doesn't seem to hold back as Cathy does when she meets a new person. We talk about his feelings, the court hearings, his parents, Cathy. "Cathy's drawn me out a lot." He is obviously very much in love with his dark-haired wife of four years because when he speaks of her his eyes soften. "We became best friends first, and our relationship is stronger because of that. We try to nurture our love for each other. Sure, we have our trials, but we're committed to our marriage.

"What counts now is that the Lord gets credit if there's any credit to be given in this story. The Lord is the one who changed Cathy's heart. He wouldn't leave her alone until she came forward with the truth. She was pretty torn up about it when she finally confessed."

"David, in all those years she did ever give any clue that she was hiding something?"

"That's hard to answer because Cathy was always moody." He shrugs, and his handsome silhouette against the light is that of a strong, rugged ironworker, a man who drives himself hard. He was a first-class gymnast in high school and in college before he dropped out to follow Cathy to New Hampshire in 1980. He's also sensitive and intelligent.

"Did you notice her going through any kind of emotional turmoil prior to her decision to recant—like temper tantrums or outbursts over seemingly small things?"

"No, I guess I don't remember anything special."

I can tell these questions bother him. Maybe he feels guilty or imperceptive. None of us like to think of ourselves as insensitive to the needs or hurts of those we love. David knows only too well that when he came home from work after ten and twelve hours on the job and commuting two and three hours to get there and back, he was in no shape to perceptively analyze anyone's behavior. He wanted to eat dinner and go to bed.

David's and Cathy's beliefs are strong, he tells me, and adds, "Marriage is an institution created by God. Cathy and I are closer now than ever before."

The drive is two hours from the airport through the city's snaking traffic to the country roads of Massachusetts and New Hampshire. We wind through forests of pine and birch, towering oak, through New England towns of white-painted houses and red-painted houses, spiked high-steepled churches, all perched amid the hills and trees of balsam, fir, and beech.

He tells me he had been to college and always expected to finish and become an engineer, but that ended when he moved to New Hampshire with Cathy. He had planned to go back and finish school while she worked, but after they were married she became pregnant and . . . well, you know how that goes.

His voice is so soft it's hard to hear him over the sound of the van's old engine. He asks me something. I don't hear him. He repeats, louder.

"Did you know Cathy's pregnant? We're so happy about it. We planned it. We'd like to have a large family." He sounds tired now. He's been up since 4:30 A.M.

"David, did you believe Cathy's story when she recanted?"

He doesn't pause before answering. "Yes."

"Did your friends and family believe her?"

"Never questioned it. You see, you had to have known Cathy. She used to be really hard. Aggressive. She got her own way no matter what it took. It wasn't difficult to believe she would do something like that —cover up a lie like that."

"So you never questioned her when she said she lied about the rape? You didn't think maybe she had flipped her lid, or that she was just feeling guilty about this guy still being in prison?"

"No."

"Did you believe her back in 1979 when she told you she *had* been raped? My math tells me that if you met in high school and you're a year older than her and you went away to college the following year, you must have been seeing each other during the trial in 1979."

"You're right. We started going together before the trial, when Dotson was convicted. I didn't really know much about it at the time and Cathy didn't want to talk about it. She told me she had been raped, though, and it really bothered me."

"Did she ever talk about the rape in the years that followed?"

"No, not really. No mention of it. I thought about it every once in a while, and I would get mad thinking of someone doing that to her. One time I was driving in the truck with my friend Mike, and a news story came on the radio about a local girl who had been raped. I got real upset thinking about Cathy. Mike asked me what was wrong, so I told him I knew a girl in high school who had been raped."

The sun is setting and the entire day seems golden. We've entered the town of Peterborough, New Hampshire, the setting for *Our Town* and the McDowell Writers Colony. We pass white wood frame houses nestled in the trees, brick factories, black smokestacks, and faded, sagging barns. I see very few people walking on the streets of the town. David and I talk the whole two hours on our ride to Jaffrey, and the time goes quickly.

"After Cathy and I got saved, our goals became the same," David is saying. "Before that, our goals were different."

I interrupt and ask him to explain what he means by "being saved."

"Well, I realized I needed God. I saw that alone I was really nothing. Even if I conquered the world, I was still nothing without God. At one time I had been interested in Eastern religion, mainly Zen. The Bible says it's by God's grace we're saved, that the way to heaven is through Jesus Christ, so I accepted Jesus Christ as my Lord. His grace saved me from a life of struggling to make philosophies work. I believe in Jesus. I've given my life over to Him. It has totally changed me because He is more than a philosophy. I have His Spirit in me to live the life He has laid out for us in His Word. It's exciting, really."

He pauses. "Even though there's been a lot of slander and Cathy's reputation is ruined, I believe she did the right thing. It's what God wanted. Cathy had to be obedient to what God wanted, no matter what the cost. That's why she came forward and confessed."

Cathy is standing at the stove; she doesn't move toward us as we enter. She smiles a half-moon smile, stirs a pot of food cooking on the stove. The small, square table in the center of the room is set for a meal.

The floors are oak, clean; all is sparkling like Mother Hubbard's kitchen. Everything is polished, bright, no dusty doorknobs here. One red rose sits in a glass in the middle of the table.

There is a huge brick fireplace, which is the first thing a visitor sees upon entering. In front of it is the wood-burning stove.

"This floor is great for the kids to ride their cars on," Cathy tells me. They're bathed and in their pajamas and are running back and forth across the floor. They jump circles around their father, who catches them in his arms and swings them through the air.

At dinner the children laugh, giggle, and chatter. The adults are quiet—self-conscious, maybe.

Cathy cuts her food up in little bites on her plate, as a mother does for her children. Then she eats slowly, lifts the tiny pieces to her mouth and chews each forkful carefully before going on to the next bite.

"We get our milk at the farm next door. A dollar and a quarter for a gallon. Want to try some?"

I politely decline the milk, as I do the Portuguese bread she offers me.

We eat in incredible silence. I can hear myself chewing and swallowing.

"A rare treat," Cathy says finally, and nods to David. He nods back. He's savoring his food, as she is, although he doesn't cut his up in tiny bites. Then Cathy mumbles something offhanded.

"Excuse me?" I say.

"I said, this is a real treat for us."

"The pot roast," David explains.

"We haven't had a roast in a long time, have we?"

"Probably not."

"Some friends from the church gave it to us. The Lord blessed them and they wanted to share it with us."

Then it hits me. She prepared a really special dinner for this occasion.

She had mentioned earlier that the pot roast was stringy. Now I understand—it wasn't idle talk, it was *important*. David and I were a whole hour late getting there. I hadn't even made a note of that. We had stopped to find a place where I could rent a car, but everything was closed up for the night and we had wasted an hour while the roast was in the oven. And to think he had only casually invited me to dinner. "Think you're too tired to stop by for something to eat?" was what he had said.

Cathy doesn't have a vacuum cleaner. It broke and she couldn't afford to buy a new one. The same is true of her dryer, the lawn mower, and the green 1973 Dodge parked in the garage.

Late that night, Cathy drives me in the van to the inn

by the lake, an old sloping, porch-wrapped place buried in the woods. She's two months pregnant, but insists on helping me carry my suitcase and typewriter up the two steep, creaking flights of stairs to my room. We say good night, and she's out the screen door, but back in about two minutes. I'm still standing at the lace-covered hall table, gathering up local newspapers and "Things to Do in New Hampshire" folders.

It's a granite-faced Cathy, like the one at the clemency hearing.

"The van won't start," she says, unruffled.

It's sitting out under the trees in the blackness, still and cold as a sunken ship at sea. She borrows a flashlight from the young man at the desk.

We trudge outside, Cathy leading the way through the dark toward the shadowy form of the dead van. There is not so much as a lemon slice of a moon to be seen. Suddenly she crouches, rolls, and is under the vehicle pulling at wires.

"Here, at least let me hold the flashlight," I offer.

"I think I got it!" Her voice is far away; she's doing something with the engine. Then out she rolls and brushes herself off. "Let's give 'er a try." Next, she's in the van, twisting the starter and shouting, "It works!" The engine grunts, chugs, and keeps chugging.

I stand there watching the red eyes of the van's taillights vanish into the trees. Turning, I feel my way back up the walk to the inn where the boy stands idly at the desk.

I hand him his flashlight. "It works," I say, and then ask, "Did you see what just happened out there?"

"Uh, no. Did something just happen?"

"Outside, just now, a pregnant woman in a *skirt* just fixed . . ." and I proceed to unravel and sift through my thoughts about this enigmatic, gentle person who only expresses what she really feels, who rolls on a country road under the belly of a bulging hulk of a van in the deadest of night. This woman with the face of a child was hurled into an international spotlight as a media symbol for recantation, and her face was splashed across the entire world as the face of a person who came forward and screamed, "He's innocent!" What I do say to the gape-mouthed boy at the desk is, "There's a light bulb out in my room," and I hop the creaking steps, down a narrow, wood-skirted hallway (which leans slightly port side) to my room.

On the Veranda at the Inn

A sprinkler shoots water across the lawn and two young students employed as gardeners stand by the railing of the veranda near us. They're talking loudly about who is going to get which day off next week. I ask Cathy if she wants to move to another spot. No, she tells me, it's nice here, she's enjoying it.

"I wanted you to see this picture," Cathy exclaims with a smile. "It's me at my confirmation. I'm thirteen. See? There's my *mother*. My mother's there. It was really special. She came to my confirmation."

She's holding the picture with both hands, almost caressing it. I move closer to look over her shoulder. The gardeners are still arguing, unable to reach a compromise.

There are three people in the picture. All three are smiling for the camera. A heavy, white-haired Nellie, in glasses and wearing a cotton shift and black slippers, sits with one arm stretched across the sofa resting on a pillow. Beside her on the sofa, squeezed in the corner, is thirteen-year-old Cathy. She's wearing a formal-length blue chiffon-and-satin dress with long, filmy sleeves and a dark-blue satin ribbon at the waist. On her feet are white flats with thick white soles. Next to her a tiny lady, thin as a sparrow, is perched on the arm of the sofa. She wears a fitted black-and-white dress, a string of pearls, and on her feet are high-heeled ankle-strap pumps.

A picture of anyone's family?

Look closer.

The old woman straddles the sofa, dominates it, legs apart, feet solidly placed on the floor. Her hand hangs loosely over her knee. She's dominant. Then there's

Cathy: Her feet are turned in, unsure, and her left hand is clenched in a small, smooth fist. Her mother is bent toward her and sits precariously on the arm of the sofa; she's on the outer edge like a bird on a twig, her thin legs tightly crossed; her left hand, like Cathy's, is clenched in a fist.

At thirteen the sense of loss was simply part of Cathy. Her mother navigated in and out of her life, the "dream" of reuniting her family traveling with her, and Cathy wanted to believe the dream would come true, but how could it? Her mother did what she thought was best to meet nice men and make the dream come true, but her prince never seemed to show up. She dreamed of a wooden cottage with white ruffled curtains, where she would have her children near her and be happy at last.

"Aunt Nellie was deteriorating," Cathy says. "She was becoming impossible. I had long before given up asking her permission to join school athletic teams or try out for cheerleading. I was needed immediately after school for housework, dinner preparation, and so on. I felt like Nellie's personal slave and her fill-in private nurse besides—administering her insulin shots and taking care of her." Cathy talks candidly now. The day is warm and easy, and we've gotten to know each other.

"As a teenager, I'd sneak out of the house after putting her to bed at night and do anything there was to do with my friends in the neighborhood. Sometimes we played kickball or softball, but mostly there were parties, boys, and getting high. Liz came along with me, but only to make sure I'd get back home all right. Another mistake on Nellie's part was that she never liked Liz because she thought she was a bad influence on me. She had that one turned around because Liz didn't drink, didn't do drugs, and she didn't have boyfriends. I was the one who was the bad influence.

"If there was a way I could thumb my nose at the world, I would. Nellie didn't know the things I did. Neither did Uncle Bill.

"I thought what I did was a real slap in the face to Nellie."

•   •   •

Cathy is looking at another picture. She points to it, rather than picking it up. It's a Polaroid shot of an attractive blond lady sitting on the lap of a handsome gray-haired man.

"That's Carol and Bernie Smith. They're the ones who got me next—my next foster parents. They took me in when Nellie got sick.

"See, after I spent two weeks with the Smiths, they decided with Aunt Nellie it would be best for me to live with them—but just five days a week because on weekends I'd have to go back to be with Nellie."

I take the picture of Bernie and Carol to look closer.

Carol Smith has an intelligent face with clear brown eyes and a defined, generous smile. She could have been a high-school homecoming queen many years back. Her husband is good-looking, strong-jawed, with deep, penetrating eyes. The photographer of this instant shot chose to place the figures at the lower half of the photo, cutting off the bottom halves of their bodies. In this way you can't see the wheelchair Bernie sits in and you can't tell that Carol isn't really sitting on his lap, but on the arm of his chair. She has her arm around him, her cheek almost resting on his head. He sits straight, upright, looking directly ahead. You can see an indication of Carol's strong, giving nature.

But Cathy didn't see that, and she wasn't willing to be parented by Carol. She still had a powerfully formed image of her fantasy mother. Perhaps Carol had imagined a fantasy daughter, too: a sweet, pink-frocked little girl who hugged and complied and would hungrily drink in the fountains of love Carol had to give. But Cathy didn't want this love—at least that's what she told herself.

It's late in the afternoon. Cathy is tired now and I can tell she wants to quit for the day. We've gone upstairs to my room to get out of the heat and glare. The room has been cool for most of the time we've been working, but now the sun has shifted and shines through the windows, snuffing out any sign of a breeze. A shaft of sunlight strikes her face and she frowns uncomfortably, shading her eyes with her hand. The air has become stifling.

The sun on Cathy's face reminds me of the hot lights of a police interrogation and perhaps that's what she is thinking, too. I get up and pull the curtain. She relaxes. She's been talking for hours, but I tell her I haven't gotten enough material to call it a day. I convince her to continue with our interview until dinner. She agrees. She pauses thoughtfully and then says, "I want you to be sure to say something good about Aunt Nellie. I think I'm painting a pretty horrible picture of her. She may have been a really nice person earlier in her life, and she was nice to me at first. I just wish she had been younger when I came to her. I know at one time she was a really good cook and she did beautiful hand sewing, too. I've seen her handiwork. I like to sew now and I could have learned a lot from her, but she was so old when I lived with her that she couldn't see to sew. Remember, by the time I moved into her house she was already losing her eyesight. She was born in 1891—can you imagine anyone giving their little four-year-old girl away to a seventy-four-year-old woman? It's still hard for me to think about—you know—about being dumped. It's hard for me to forgive my father.

"Anyhow, about lying. Well, I *had* to lie. It was the only way to get what I wanted. After that first visit of my mother's, I told Nellie it didn't matter if she came to see me or not. I thought if I lied maybe she'd agree to let her come again. I didn't know where my mother lived or how to find her. Nellie controlled my whole world."

Cathy speaks in halting sentences and often interrupts herself in the middle of a thought. Sometimes she drops the end of a statement as if the listener already knew what she was going to say.

"I started to tell you about how I began experimenting sexually. I started pretty young—at about twelve—with a neighbor boy. But I never felt bad or guilty about those experiences. I enjoyed the attention, I suppose. I mean, Aunt Nellie never hugged or touched, and I don't ever remember anyone telling me "I love you'' when I was young. Those sexual experiences gave me something to be good at, or at least that's what I told myself. And I felt sort of loved. Stupid, isn't it?''

I try to imagine her at twelve years old. She's a package of unresolved conflicts, and sexuality is one of them. Because her sexual development was never discussed, as love was not, she had no understanding of it. Aunt Nellie seemed to have no sexuality. Her body was a creature of its own, an aging shell invaded by illness. But Cathy's body was growing up, developing, as is God's design for every growing person. Cathy saw sex as a substitute for love, because she had no frame of reference for either.

Nellie projected the attitude that sex was the secret dread of womanhood. She often said it was what a woman gave—no, *sacrificed*—to a man. Sex was bad. To be lovely, appealing, to have any physical contact with the opposite sex was bad. Cathy's developing body was a curse, a thing to be embarrassed about. "Don't wear that dress, it shows your body," was said, not of a tasteless, too-tight outfit, but of a dress with a fitted waist. The message Cathy received was that the body she lived in was becoming an evil, dangerous thing.

I shuffle through the pages of Cathy's scrapbook and come up with a photograph that looks like a ten-year-old Cathy. A sweet, round-faced girl looks up at me from the picture—a girl with a dimpled smile and pale, white skin. Her dark hair is combed neatly, with the ends carefully curled under.

"I hate that picture," she says immediately. "I hated that dress—Nellie made me wear it."

The picture hardly shows the dress, except for the collar. "You can't even see the dress," I point out. "This is a head shot."

"Well, *I* know I'm wearing it. Can't you tell I'm unhappy? I'm actually gritting my teeth."

I study the photograph more closely. Why can't I tell she's gritting her teeth? My first impression is that this child could be anyone's little sister, niece, or cousin. She's a ten-year-old who looks like other ten-year-olds, plays the same games as other ten-year-olds, laughs at the same jokes, learns the same lessons in school, lies the same lies. . . .

But no, she's a ten-year-old quite unlike most. First, trust was never formed in her infant development. Then perceptions developed through confusion and fear: Who would love her? Where was her house? Would the ghosts get her for being bad? At first her anger frightened her so she could only turn it inward and cry. Then the anger took over as her only defense against a hostile world. Cathy knows about the grinding teeth: her anger is a permanent photograph in her mind.

This ten-year-old is at a major crossroad of life. She is about to leave her younger, compliant self in exchange for a more defiant one.

Aunt Nellie taught her that sex was bad, not with words so much as by behavior, by her own attitude and opinions of herself and her femininity. Nellie's forms of sex education were admonitions such as, "Stay away from boys" and "Stop roughhousing with Uncle Bill!" When Nellie told Bill, "It's not right for her to be sitting on your lap or wrestling like that," Bill just stopped those things and never explained why to Cathy. It made her feel unclean.

One lesson Nellie gave to Cathy was that the world was dangerous. But Cathy saw no dangers in the outside world and so she believed Nellie was depriving her of enjoying life. Another lesson was that Cathy was fragile, incapable of handling danger, and vulnerable to evil ways (what she needed was to be taught the skills of living in a dangerous world). The emphasis was on shame. So when Cathy became promiscuous right under Nellie's nose, it wasn't her own body she thought she defamed, it was Nellie's.

She had always told Nellie what she thought Nellie wanted to hear and she did what Nellie expected of her. In this way she learned to associate lying with acceptance and approval.

"There's another thing I haven't told you about. That's the time I tried to murder Nellie."

"Murder Aunt Nellie?"

"I didn't feel any guilt about that, either. After I turned ten I stopped being the perfect little girl. Nellie was getting older and her health was getting worse. I had to give her her baths and I cooked most of the meals with her sitting at the table supervising me. I deliberately would do things wrong to get her angry. She had me shampoo and set her hair and I would fix it the opposite of what she wanted. It would make her furious but there wasn't a thing she could do about it. Should I tell you how I tried to murder her?"

I close the scrapbook and stand the little photograph on the dresser against the mirror.

"How about we eat dinner first?" The sweet-faced ten-year-old gritting her teeth calls to me, and I want her to know someone is here and listening.

10

Beverly Hills
1971-1975

AFTER NELLIE GOT custody of me, I saw a program on
TV where an old lady was murdered by her niece. That's
where I got the idea. I began a childish plan of how I
would do it and when the day came, I was ready. I
brought her a cup of coffee laced with some harmful-
looking powder I got from the medicine cabinet. I was
shaking so much when I handed the cup to her, I accidentally dropped the tray with her food. She snapped
her usual "You can't do anything right!" and she drank
the coffee. I went back to the kitchen to fix her another
tray of food. I was numb. I felt absolutely nothing. I
thought for certain when I returned to her room she
would be dead.

What happened was, she gulped down the coffee and
then followed it up with a full breakfast and went to
sleep. She woke up with diarrhea and that was all there
was to it. She was hardly even sick. I was defeated
again. Nellie still controlled me.

On my way out of the room I paused to look at the
photos under the glass top of her dresser. Her sons,
Fran, Charlie, and the son who died as a policeman,

were there under the glass, as well as her grandsons
Mark and David; and there was Carol and Bernie . . .
they were all smiling out from under the glass.

There were pictures of long-dead relatives, ancient,
worn pictures of people from another world. I wasn't
really looking for anything, just sort of gazing at
Nellie's little family museum. I didn't expect to find a
picture of myself among them, and I didn't.

A miracle happened and my mother started coming
around about once a month. Aunt Nellie didn't like it
one bit but she let her come anyhow. I couldn't help but
wonder if my mother didn't get some kind of legal
visiting rights. We took the bus to the pancake house on
Western Avenue for lunch. Nellie didn't try to stop us,
but my mother could only have me for two hours, ". . .
exactly, not a minute longer," so she was nervous all
through lunch, smoked a pack of cigarettes, and then I
got nervous, too. "We just *can't* miss that bus," she
would say. I would feel helpless and afraid because it
was scary to see that my mother was as afraid as I was. I
didn't want to miss the bus either. I'd be punished and
not able to go out with my mother the next time. I didn't
want to have to sit on a chair across the room from her
like we used to. It had been three years since I'd seen
her. I never wanted to lose my mother. I don't know
why, but I didn't tell her that.

When we were alone, she'd take my hand. She was
very affectionate and I felt uncomfortable and embarrassed. It was such a nice touch, not mean or gruff. She
touched me a lot. She stroked and squeezed and hugged
and put her arm around me; she tapped her fingers on
my arm. When we walked she always wanted to hold my
hand. But I wasn't used to affection and I didn't know
how to act.

My mother had a dream she told me about every time
we were together. She loved her dream and I wanted to
believe it.

Sometimes she cried when she told me the dream, and

she held my hands real tight. I sat very stiff and pretended my face was made of wood so I wouldn't cry, too.

"I have this dream," she would tell me, "that I'll be married again to a real nice man who loves me and loves you, too. He'll love us both very much and take care of us, and he'll be thankful I have such a wonderful daughter. We won't be apart anymore. Nothing will ever take you away from me again. We'll live in a pretty wooden house, like a cottage in the country. There will be white ruffled curtains on the windows. The wood floors will be clean and shiny, and you'll have a bedroom all your own. You'll bring your friends home after school and I'll serve chocolate chip cookies and milk and we'll be so happy. That's my dream, that we'll be together again."

And then she would see my face and her own would break, like little pieces of a puzzle. She would start to cry. "Cathy, why do you look at me like that? Your face is so cold and hard—it makes me think you don't believe me!"

She never understood I was trying not to cry.

There's a flat, gray stretch of stores and commercial buildings along Western Avenue. For me it suddenly gained color when my mother was at my side. The low-topped buildings stood taller, brighter, because *she* was with me, and the homely shops looked far less forlorn to me. The whole world was happier, in fact. But nothing good lasts (we were *positive* the bus came earlier than scheduled), and we were fifteen minutes late getting back to Nellie's.

Nellie punished me for being late, and it would be weeks, maybe months, before my mother would show up again at the front door. Again we would be planted across the room from each other, fidgeting nervously and saying dumb things. Aunt Nellie presided from her big green chair in the corner, and then the visit was over, and my mother was gone.

Liz was there one afternoon when my mother came to

see me, and she sat on the arm of my chair fidgeting right along with me. I don't know who was more nervous—Liz, my mother, or me.

"Your mother is nice," Liz said feebly after Mother was gone.

"Yeah. . . ."

"I mean, she's just like a person's mother."

"Well, Nellie thinks she's a bad person."

At that moment, Nellie was in the doorway, pulling apart the curtains that separated my room from the living room. "Keep this curtain open, young lady." I knew what that meant. If I had a friend in my room the curtain had to be open because Nellie thought I was a bad person, too.

It was so confusing. At night I did what I had promised myself I would never do again. I hated myself for it, but I couldn't help it. I *cried*. I prayed to God and asked Him, "Why am I here? Why did You let me be born?"

Then one day I resolved to make things easier on everybody by committing suicide. If I were dead they'd all be happier. It was a Saturday afternoon and Uncle Bill wasn't home. I knew he wouldn't be home until late. Nellie was in her bed going over papers with a magnifying glass. I decided the time was perfect so I went into the bathroom and pulled out a bottle of Aunt Nellie's pills from the medicine cabinet. I downed them all.

I wasn't concerned about what I should wear or how I wanted to be found after I was dead. These things didn't matter. I had already swallowed the pills. I sure wasn't going to change clothes now. I decided I'd just sit down at the kitchen table and turn on the TV and wait. Just when I was beginning to feel groggy, Aunt Nellie yelled from her room, "Cathy, will you bring me a cup of coffee?"

Sure, sure. I hoped I'd drop dead on the way. I boiled the water and just as I was pouring the coffee into the cup, the world tipped on its side, and I went with it, tumbling, crashing, and dropping off the edge.

• • •

"Cathleen Crowell! are you deaf?"

I awoke on the floor of the kitchen in total darkness except for the flashing, moving reflections of the TV screen against the wall. Thickheaded, nauseous, and dizzier than I had ever been in my life, I stumbled into the bathroom, where I spent most of the rest of the night. Aunt Nellie never found out why her coffee didn't arrive, and she didn't mention it.

I figured it was just bad luck. I couldn't even kill myself.

The next day I baked Aunt Nellie some biscuits and lathered them with blueberry jam and then slept and slept. Soon after that I began to think about running away. But if I did I'd miss my mother when she came for me. That worried me.

Everything worried me. There were so many thoughts in my mind about so many different things. I wished I weren't developing so fast. I was different from all the other girls I knew. They were still wearing undershirts, but Uncle Bill handed me a bra and said I should start wearing it. How embarrassing! Was it my fault I was growing up? Aunt Nellie acted as if she didn't have the slightest idea what it was all about. What did it mean to be a female anyway?

By the time my eighth-grade graduation came along I felt like an old woman. I baked a cake and made a big pot of coffee for the party at Nellie's house. Uncle Bill's brother Bob and his wife Jean came. So did Carol and Bernie. Aunt Nellie was being decent. I opened presents. Uncle Bill had already given me a suitcase for the trip to Washington with my class. He even paid for the entire trip himself so I could go. Aunt Nellie never mentioned the trip. Even after I returned with three rolls of film of the White House and the Washington Monument, plus one more roll of the kids on the bus, she acted as if she didn't want to hear me talk about it. That usually meant she was mad at me. Uncle Bill would do the same if he got mad at me for talking back or misbehaving. He wouldn't talk to me for sometimes two weeks. Why? It made me feel so bad.

Nellie said my problem was that I took advantage of her, but I got back at her for saying that, so it didn't matter. I heard her talking to Carol one day and telling her what a trial I was. A *trial*.

I got even with Aunt Nellie by stealing money from her drawer. Liz and I ate loads of cotton candy, thanks to Aunt Nellie's stash of change and bills in her drawer. I wondered if she got suspicious because after a while she didn't trust me with her church offering envelopes anymore. (She didn't go to church, but she sent me.) Could I help it if she tucked cash in the envelopes? Liz and I had hot dogs by the truckful with the money from those little envelopes. But then the church mailed out a letter telling people how much they gave each year. Aunt Nellie sealed checks in the envelopes after that.

My father didn't come to my graduation. It was a disappointment. I thought maybe he might at least have written, so I hunted through Nellie's drawers for a letter or something from him, but the checks that did come in once in a while didn't have a return address. I reread an old letter from him, my eyes fixed on the words "Give Cathy a hug and tell her I love her. One day I hope she'll understand. . . ." I closed the drawer.

Now I really hated him.

11

Beverly Hills and Homewood
1975

I REMEMBER THE first time Nellie went into a coma. It was not too long before I moved in with Carol and Bernie. Nellie had diabetes, but she still loved to eat. She would get up in the middle of the night and have cookies and jams and jellies.

The day stands out in my mind because in the afternoon we had had a big fight. I screamed at her because she wouldn't let me go outside to play. She told me she was doing me a big favor by allowing me to live there. I was in the house with her, taking care of her, cleaning; *trapped*, while the other kids were out having fun. I wanted to be a kid, too. I didn't know anybody whose parents threatened to send them to a State detention home just for talking back. I figured *real* parents didn't even think about detention homes.

I was angry and kept thinking about running away. I ran out of the house crying and headed for Liz's. She comforted me and talked me out of leaving. She reminded me of the lady down the block who often had offered to adopt me to get me away from Aunt Nellie.

As Liz later put it, "Nellie found out about that and she flew into such a rage, I thought the top of her head would fly right off and land in her vaporizer."

When I went back home I called her but she didn't answer. At first I thought she was asleep. I shook her, patted her cheek—nothing. I was confused and didn't know what to do, so I called Carol and Bernie's house. They reached a doctor, who sent an ambulance, and when the ambulance arrived I was sitting in the chair next to Aunt Nellie, who was white as a blank piece of paper. Now I felt as though her life were in my hands; I feared she would get me back if something horrible happened to her.

Carol and Bernie decided I shouldn't stay in the house alone that night. Nellie would need to be hospitalized, so they brought me home with them. I tried to convince them I wasn't alone, Uncle Bill would be there, but later Nellie insisted I stay with them.

Bernie's calm personality prevailed over the Smith household. I almost forgot he was in a wheelchair because he never complained. He was friendly toward me, talked to me, and listened when I talked. Carol had her "schedule" and she was uptight a lot of the time. But they didn't scream or fight—and they didn't yell at me, either.

On the Fourth of July, Carol and Bernie held a family barbecue in the backyard. Carol served a special birthday cake for Mark and David, whose birthdays fall within a couple of weeks of July 4, and for me, since my birthday is June 26. I should have felt included when I saw my name with David's and Mark's, but to me it looked sort of sad. I was certain Carol thought I was in the way—maybe just because they were related to Nellie. When Carol handed me a beautifully wrapped birthday present, I figured she was just trying to make me feel good. It didn't occur to me that she really cared.

The Smith house was immaculate. There was a place for everything. No papers flying around like at Aunt Nellie's, and no nooks and crannies filled with junk and old collections of string, bags, bottles, store coupons, *TV Guides*, and extension cords. Carol outlined a list of duties immediately so I knew what was expected of me. "Everyone has their share of duties on the weekly schedule and you'll be no exception," she announced. I think it was supposed to make me feel like one of them.

My job on the schedule was to clear the dishes after dinner, an easy job. I didn't have to prepare dinner, wash dishes, clean the kitchen, or wait on Aunt Nellie. It was like having no job at all. I was afraid to ask if I could go out afterward so I just sat in a chair, as I did day after day at Aunt Nellie's, and behaved as I thought I should. I didn't laugh, joke, or say anything. I just sat with my eyes glued to the TV. Finally, after nearly a week of this, I mustered the courage to stand in the doorway of the living room and interrupt the "Wonderful World of Disney" with, "Is it all right if I go outside for a while?" I was ready with a list of reasons, lies to tell them, if necessary, about how I simply *had* to go out and watch the neighbor kids play ball in the field out back.

Both Carol and Bernie casually looked up, nodded, and said, "Sure, have fun."

I was shocked.

I didn't want to stay there for long, even though it was peaceful and they didn't make me beg to go out. All I knew was I had to get out of Aunt Nellie's and I was going to do it one way or another. I wasn't sure where I wanted to live. I only knew I didn't want to go to the State.

The Smiths were building a new house on Ridge Road in Homewood, a brick house on an enormous lot right across from a park. Aunt Nellie gave permission for me to move in with them. They altered the walls of two of the bedrooms and made one bigger for the two boys to share and the other smaller for me. I knew I should be grateful, but my heart was cold. This wasn't my real home and these people weren't my real family. They probably just felt sorry for me the way a person feels sorry for a stray cat.

I knew Nellie had complained about me to Carol, so it was sort of like being dropped off for dinner by my father all over again. ("Cathy's a bad, bad girl. I hope you can handle her.")

Numb. Yes, that describes it. At Nellie's I had cried at night and asked God why He ever let me be born. I had asked it a thousand times; now I didn't care.

With my responsibilities clearly explained and defined for me, it was easy to do what was expected of me. It was strange, at first, to finish my list of duties and then be able to go out. I felt as if I were getting away with something. At Nellie's, every time I finished one job, she had another waiting for me. I'd say, "I finished the kitchen, may I go out now and play?" and she'd say, "Do the bathroom." At Carol and Bernie's, when I finished doing the work on my list, that was it. Clean my room, set the table, clear the table (one week out of every three), wash the basement stairs, and dust the dining room . . . and no more. It felt peculiar not to have to lie or sneak out. I liked the feeling, even though I didn't trust it.

In the fall of 1975 I started my freshman year at Homewood-Flossmoor High School. It was a huge place with many buildings. Roads and paths and walkways led from one building to another. There were little park areas, recreational areas, and every kind of tree and plant imaginable, all on ninety-eight acres of land. My classes were in buildings lettered *A* through *H*, and another building called the North building. I couldn't imagine how I was going to get from one building to another in the ten short minutes we had between classes. The halls in the buildings were wide, the floors gleaming and polished. There were cases of trophies lining the walls and a confusing system of numbered rooms. When the bell rang, a stampede of human bodies came crashing through the halls, dispersing in every direction. One time I looked up and saw what I thought was a herd of buffalo galloping at me, so I quickly turned around and ran with them in the direction they were running. It took me ten minutes to find my way back to where I had started.

I was the new kid again. With no friends, no one to talk to, alone in that sprawling metropolis of a school, I was more than frightened: I was without feeling. It was like that first school Nellie had sent me to where I had become a nonperson in a strange and alien place. I didn't see one of those thousands of bodies as a real person. Back in Beverly, at least, I had an idea of who I was because there I understood my place and I identified with Liz and my little group of misfits. Here it was like not having a self. I remembered when I first ventured out of Nellie's yard, I was worried I wouldn't exist anymore. I had that same feeling when I started high school.

And yet I hated going back to Beverly on the weekends. Maybe it was a feeling from another time, like being transferred from Daddy's place to Mommy's place, back and forth—I could almost hear myself crying and clinging to my father's pant leg. It was the teenage equivalent of wanting my Cuddly Dudley.

That was how I felt now: back and forth, back and forth, from the Smiths to Nellie Landers. I felt rootless; there was nothing for me to love.

One day I was out in the backyard and Bill was at the garbage cans throwing bags of old things away. I saw my little stove and refrigerator set going in the garbage and I called out, "What are you doing? Those are mine!"

"This is only junk—"

"But they were from my father! He gave them to me!"

I sat down on the bottom stair in the basement, too sad to cry.

After one weekend at Nellie's I returned to the Smiths to learn they had just come back from a family outing to

Cantigny War Museum. Without me. I had never been more than a guest on a family outing in my life. It was one of the things I dreamed about. From that time on I was convinced the reason I had to go to Nellie's was so the Smiths could be rid of me and have time for their "own" family without me. I didn't believe them when they said I was part of the family. I didn't want to call them Mom and Dad, because they weren't. But it seemed to mean a lot to them, so I did. I wanted to avoid conflict.

The thing is, I really wanted to be the Smiths' perfect daughter. It was like a goal, a drive to be part of someone's family. If I could be perfect, maybe they'd love me. Maybe they'd feel more comfortable with me around. Maybe Carol would be like a mom and do the things that moms do—share clothes with her daughter, hug me for no reason at all, tell me how good I was doing, and how happy she was I was there. I concentrated hard on my schoolwork because if I got good grades, they might be proud of me and brag about me.

But of course, the roof had to cave in on me.

One of the boys I met at a party in Beverly wrote me some torrid letters about his sexual fantasies—in detail. I had been sexually involved with him but we hadn't had intercourse. He was continuing where we left off. These letters were really flaming, and I would have been embarrassed if I hadn't thought they were funny. Liz and I figured he had copied everything out of some pornographic magazine. I made the mistake of hiding them in the drawer of the nightstand by my bed, and Carol found them. Why was she going through my things while I was at Nellie's? But when Carol and Bernie picked me up to drive me back to Homewood, it was strangely silent in the car. Then I saw that Carol had the letters in her fist. She tried to be very controlled as Bernie talked about the letters.

When I got back to their house, I discovered my room was torn apart: clothes, books, underwear, shoes, trinkets, whatever little memorabilia I had was thrown everywhere. Even my bedding was pulled apart. I begged them to believe that the letters were only the boy's fantasies. I would have pleaded with Carol to believe me, but then I saw my room and thought, *What's the use?* Bernie said they would forget about it and never mention it again.

Nearly ten years later, at a nationally televised Illinois Prison Review Board clemency hearing, before the governor of Illinois, Carol brought those letters up again. They hadn't believed me.

12

1977

MY WEEKENDS AT Aunt Nellie's were all the same. They melted into one another like one long camphor-smelling, overheated experience. I wanted to be a teen-ager and have fun like everybody else.

If I was in summer school I brought my books to study. I studied all the time when I was taking classes. But when school was over, I could put the schoolbooks aside and read my favorite romance books.

Nellie's house was musty smelling, acrid, and the familiar odors of camphor and stale air hit me as I stood in the doorway of her kitchen. Carol was already inside, tossing her purse on the table. It was Friday afternoon, and she was dropping me off at my weekend prison. She called cheerily, "Nana! We're here!" Then turning to me, still standing in the doorway, she admonished, "Come on, you'll let the flies in."

I closed the screen door behind me and placed my books on the floor by the table. I sagged at the thought of the weekend and flopped into a chair.

Carol was always loving and affectionate with Aunt Nellie, babying her and talking loudly, as if her ears were stuffed with paper. "Are you *sure* you have enough of everything, Nana? How are you doing for

stockings? Looks like you'll be needing new slippers!
Do you have enough underwear? What did the doctor
say yesterday? How are your legs today? Any more
itching? Do you want the *TV Guide*? Here, let me fix
that pillow for you!"

Nauseating. Nellie almost purred! She was so grateful
and sweet to Carol. But for me, who traipsed over there
every weekend and didn't get to go to the football games
or Friday-night dances, not so much as a thanks. She
had sons of her own to take care of her in her old age,
and they did help out (and she loved them for it, too),
but who got stuck on weekends and who helped her
cook and clean and anything else she needed? Yours
truly.

Here I was, sixteen years old, and Nellie still treated
me as if I were a five-year-old who couldn't reach the
other side of the street without her flagging me across.
She had to monitor my every minute when I was at her
house. If I left in the morning to go meet Liz, I couldn't
go out later. If I went out in the afternoon for a couple
of hours, I couldn't go out at night; if I went out in the
evening I couldn't go out at all during the day. It was in-
sane. There was nothing to do but read my romance
books.

The weight of his body held her . . . Heather began
to fight . . . she sought to scratch or claw him . . .
but always a hand or elbow was there to stem her
effort. He laughed. . . .

"Nana! I'm leaving! Cathy, be sure to fix Nana some
lunch."

"Uh-huh."

"Say, what are you reading?" I held up the book so
she could see the cover. I continued reading the perils of
Heather.

"Oh, yes. I read that one. Well, bye."

At last his grip slackened and she could breathe . . .

*an imprint of his fingers was clearly marked upon
her fair skin. . . .*

"I'm hungry, Cathy. Is it time for lunch?"
I opened the cupboard door. Nellie loved lunch. The
best time of the day for Nellie was when she could eat; it
gave her something to do. I stared disinterestedly into
the cupboard when suddenly the sight of a two-pound
box of brown sugar behind boxes of cereal and soda
crackers hit my eye. I felt a familiar tug from somewhere far away. I vaguely remembered the brick house
in Worth, Illinois. *Hot, muggy air. Closed windows.
Darkened kitchen. Smoke, choking air, Mama!* The
feeling was so surprising, I closed my eyes and took a
deep breath. I didn't want to remember, didn't want to
think about painful things. I hated to have to think
about things that hurt.
"How about tuna salad, Aunt Nellie?" I asked
quickly, to divert my attention.
"That will be fine, and I think I'll have a little jam on
the side."
"Me, too." And next to the jam, I poured a little
bowl of brown sugar, just to dip with a tiny bit of water.

That day was spent listlessly cleaning, doing laundry,
taking care of Nellie's hundreds of needs, and in order
to break the tedium, reading my romance paperback.

*. . . she became like a wild thing . . . biting, clawing
at him. Yet he only laughed. . . .*

When Nellie finally took her afternoon nap, the heat
seemed to compress the rooms of that house, crushing
everything inside, including me. I knew I'd suffocate if I
didn't get out of there, so without asking permission, I
took a walk over to Liz's house.
Each summer the high old oak trees made green arch-
ways across the streets of Beverly. I walked slowly along
the familiar sloping sidewalk with its patches and grassy

cracks. In a way I missed this old neighborhood, though it didn't quite feel like mine anymore now that I lived in Homewood during the week. Liz and I went to different schools, lived far apart, and maybe we wouldn't be as close anymore. She would find another best friend. I quickly put the thought out of my mind. I'd think about something else.

"Let's go shopping," Liz suggested. "I still owe you a birthday present. We can go to the mall and—"

I stopped her. "I have to get back. Nellie will miss me if she wakes up and finds me gone."

"How about later?"

"I'll ask."

"Don't just ask, *beg*."

"That's what asking means, doesn't it?"

Aunt Nellie was awake when I returned, perspiring and clattering around in the kitchen.

"Where were you?"

"I went to the store. I was gone two minutes, that's all."

"What did you buy at the store?"

"A can of pop. I was thirsty."

"What's wrong with the pop in the refrigerator?"

"Well, I wanted a different kind."

"That's just an excuse to go gallivanting around, that's all."

"Aunt Nellie, I was only gone exactly *two* minutes, honest."

"It takes more than two minutes just to get to the store. I wasn't born yesterday."

"Well, you see, I didn't get all the way there because I forgot my money, so I came back to—"

"You forgot? I swear, you'd forget your—"

What could I tell her that she'd believe? She refused to release me to the outside world!

I called Liz and told her I'd "beg" again tomorrow. I was furious, and that was something new. I had been so docile all those years and now I just couldn't take it anymore: "Aunt Nellie, I'm like a prisoner here."

"Well, you can go out after you finish your chores."

Nothing worked. I knew I'd be doing chores all day. I couldn't imagine what Aunt Nellie was afraid of. What on earth did she think could possibly happen to me outside her house?

Friday night as Aunt Nellie and Uncle Bill watched "M*A*S*H" on TV, I sat slouched in the gray chair in the living room, reading.

But now she knew differently. She was going to have a baby—a baby by that scoundrel of a sea captain. That cad! Madman! Lunatic! Oh, God, she thought, why? Why?

Livid with rage, Aunt Fanny shook Heather until her head threatened to snap off. "Who is it? Who's the bloody toad?" she cried. The old aunt's hands tightened around Heather's arms until it brought an outcry of pain from the girl's lips. . . .

"Cathy, will you please change the channel?"

Before putting Aunt Nellie to bed that night, I sprinkled and rubbed talcum powder on her body to cool her off and gave a few quick brush strokes to her hair. I wasn't particularly gentle about it. "Tomorrow, Cathy, I want you to shampoo and set my hair. This heat—it makes me sticky all over."

"Yeah, these days are real scorchers," I replied, and I decided to ask her then about going out with Liz tomorrow. "Is it all right if I'm gone a couple of hours in the afternoon tomorrow?"

A demanding eye shot up at me. "What for?"

Automatically as clockwork I answered, "It's sort of a surprise. I shouldn't tell you, but if you really want to know, it's Carol's idea. She asked me to buy you a pair of slippers—to surprise you."

"I don't need slippers."

"Carol says you do. You don't want to hurt Carol's feelings, do you?"

"I'll call Carol and see about this."

"Too bad, she wanted it to be a surprise."

Saturday Liz and I went shopping, but unfortunately for me, I wasn't back on time so Nellie grounded me for the rest of my stay. (I think what really ticked her off was that I forgot the slippers.)

I stretched across my bed and read almost an entire book while eating buttered slices of white bread and drinking milk.

Sometimes they had their secret, stolen meetings in the abandoned warehouse where it had all begun, and sometimes . . . in her own bedroom, late at night. But he never spent a night with her—never stayed longer than an hour or two at most. . . .

I hated going to Nellie's. I hated Nellie's airless house, Nellie's sickness, Nellie's rules. My only diversion was reading.

They tied the lantern to the side of the wagon and threw her onto the ground beside it . . . eyes glaring down into hers, laughter. . . .

It was late and I could hear the crickets outside in the yard and the sound of Aunt Nellie in her room, rolling and muttering from her bed.

The girl had bruises all over her body—there was a livid blue mark on her cheekbone . . . and her lip bled, but she kept right on struggling . . . like a hurt animal.

"Cathy, why is the light on? Are the kids sleeping? Who's not in bed? Charlie?"

Exasperated, I placed the book facedown and went into Nellie's room to calm her. "You're having a nightmare, Aunt Nellie," I called to her. Her night-light was on, and I could see she had twisted the sheet around her body; she was soaked with perspiration. I placed my hand on her forehead and at that instant her own hot, moist hand folded over mine.

"Cathy, is that you?" she murmured.

"Yes, Aunt Nellie, you were having a nightmare."

"Cathy, I—"

"How come you turned the fan off, Aunt Nellie? It's like an oven in here. Let me fix this sheet for you."

She held my hand in her grip. "Thank you," she said loud and clear, her fingers squeezing mine. She looked right at me when she said it, as though both weak eyes, shrunken without her glasses, could see me. I didn't catch any meaning in this gesture at all; in fact, I ignored it.

"Cathy, I want to—I—"

"Aunt Nellie, can't I please open a window in here? It's *roasting*."

It had never occurred to me, not once, that Nellie might have loved my presence in the house, or that she might have needed *me*, wanted *me*. I always thought she just *needed*.

So I went back to my book while Nellie lay in her bed, straining to see the faint light my lamp cast across the living-room floor, with tears, like transparent silk, filming the corners of two dimmed eyes.

The following days of the summer of 1977 were to change my life and the lives of many innocent people for ill because of the lie I told about being raped. After many hours of testimony and many more hours being interviewed for this book, I am not able to fully recall or reconstruct the events of those days. Few people would have total recall of every event on a particular day eight years earlier, even an important day. Many people remember various details of their wedding day, but not of the day preceding or the day following.

In my case, the events preceding the night I was intimate with David Beirne, a boy from the neighborhood in Beverly, blur because there was nothing distinctive about them; rather, they had the same boring regularity of times I spent at Nellie's house. Two things I remember with certainty: (1) the fear that the sex act I engaged in with David might make me pregnant and (2)

the rape I faked by scratching and disfiguring myself in
Aquilla Park on the night of July 9, 1977.

It has been pointed out to me that forgetting is also
part of the pattern of the antisocial personality I had as
a teenager. Painful events, times, people, and places
were blurred or blotted from my memory as my conscious mind sought to defend itself against loss and rejection. In psychological terms this behavior is known
as *disassociation*. But I was not wiping a rape, a gang
rape, or any other such event from my mind as some
people have theorized.

I do not have a blank spot in my mind about being
raped. I remember tearing my clothes and faking the appearance of a rape victim. I knew from July 9 on that I
was lying about being raped. My memory lapses now
are due to the passage of time and the terror I felt then
at having to create and then maintain an elaborate lie to
people in authority. It had to be some process of mind
that made me able to look at an innocent person and ac-
cuse him of rape, without any guilt or regard for him at
all. That cruel scene and all the events connected with it
are the events that my mind tried to erase. I knew I was
lying, but I couldn't admit it.

The account that follows is what took place on those
days in July as near as I can now reconstruct it: In the
summer of 1977 I attended the first semester of summer
school, which started June 20 and ended July 8. After
school let out at half-past twelve, I headed for Aunt
Nellie's. I arrived, tired, hot, and thirsty, to find her sitting at the kitchen table waiting for me. She was pleasant for a change, and I was glad because after taking
two final exams that morning, I was in no mood to fight
with her.

Her face lit up when I fixed lunch and after I helped
her into bed for her nap, I stretched across my bed and
picked up a romance book and read it.

Later I went out shopping. I rode my bike to the
Jewel on 103rd Street, past the flower store, the den-
tist's office, and the teen fashion store. On my way back
I decided to ride around the neighborhood to see if I

could find any of my friends. I saw a couple of guys I knew walking along Wood Avenue. One of them was a boy named David Beirne. He and I had been intimate. I rode my bike close to the curb and slowed down.

We started talking and after a while we made arrangements for him to come over after Aunt Nellie went to bed. I wasn't sure I liked the boy. I didn't think he really liked me. Our relationship wasn't much more than sexual.

We had been having sex on and off for the past year. Even though we didn't know each other as people, I thought the affair gave me the affection I was looking for.

Around eleven Nellie and Uncle Bill went to their rooms. The house was dark and I sat on the edge of my bed with my heart pounding a mile a minute. My window was open and any minute he would be out there. If Nellie heard him, that would be the end of me. I didn't know what she'd do if she caught a boy in my bed.

There was nothing romantic about these little visits. We had never dated, didn't talk—he had never even said he liked me. He was just a boy, and I was just—well, I was *there*. Then I heard him. "Sshh," I warned through the screen, and I let him in the front door. As usual we didn't even look at each other, just tiptoed to my bedroom and closed the curtain behind us. We were always very quiet. I think the only words we spoke that night were before he rose to leave. I asked him if he had been careful as we'd agreed on. He said yes, but I was sure he hadn't been. I was sure he had ejaculated in me.

After he left I lay quite still, listening to the sound of the crickets. What if he had made me pregnant? I was only sixteen! *Pregnant! How could he?* I barely slept that night.

13

July 9, 1977

EARLY SATURDAY MORNING I woke up worrying. *What if I'm pregnant?* I forced myself out of bed, pulled on the rest of my clothes, and met Nellie in the doorway. She needed at least a hundred more things done before I left to go back to Homewood. I had almost forgotten I had to work that night at Long John Silver's. I had only been working there a short time and I'd have to get back in time to change into my uniform. I felt like calling in sick, but I knew I couldn't.

Pregnant. What would I do? I could see myself helpless and wiped out. I'd have to leave high school just when things were going well for me. Carol and Bernie would probably send me to a State detention home. I'd be finished.

I probably asked Uncle Bill to give me a ride back to Homewood, though Carol usually picked me up. I couldn't stand the thought of riding in the car with Carol, knowing I could be pregnant. She was the one I feared the most. She had such high moral standards: those awkward little talks of hers about how a girl's greatest asset was her virginity and how a girl should keep herself for that one special person. Well, it was too late for me. I wish she could have been around when I was younger. If she knew all about me, she'd be horrified. She'd have a screaming fit and kick me out. I'd go straight to the State, quicker than anything.

How could I go to work in this frame of mind? *I'll drop things all over the place.* I was sick to my stomach. How could guys be so stupid? How could I? *Carol will ask me what's wrong. If I act funny, she'll think I'm sick and she'll question me.* I would have to be cautious so she wouldn't notice anything different about me. *Act normal. Don't draw attention to yourself.*

The whole day was a tangle, a fog; I couldn't focus on a thing around me. Once home I got dressed for work. *Put on the uniform, get the apron, comb your hair, put on some lipstick.* They would take the baby from me and put it up for adoption. I wouldn't have anywhere to go, my life would be over. *Put on your socks, the navy knee-highs. Try to relax. Try to act natural.*

I sat on my bed, looking at the room in its pinkness and little-girl frothiness, and I realized it wasn't a room for me at all. I couldn't even remember being a little girl. Now what? What next? *What do I do?* Time literally stopped for me that moment; I just knew I was pregnant. I wanted to get out of the house as fast as I could.

The hours I worked at Long John Silver's passed in a blur. Movement and sounds ran together like a frenzied montage: voices all talking at once; faces, a fat man with a bald head, a lady with a tie-dyed headband, four junior-high kids slapping the counter with straws, a baby crying; lines of bodies at the counter; tables filled with bodies; chewing mouths at every table; grease spattering; laughter. "One Fish and Fries Dinner!" "Two Fish & More Dinners!" *Need more fries; bus the front;* "Keg of slaw!" *Bus the front;* "Three Cokes—hold the ice!"

Socks rolling down into my shoes. "Bring out more Hush Puppies!" "Sweep this up, will you!" "Where are the fries?" "Another keg of slaw!" Smoke, clouds of it; "Are we out of Hush Puppies?" *Help me, somebody help me, please.* Whispering, piped-in music;

"Don't you just hate Saturdays in this place?" "Cathy, check to see if we're out of Hush Puppies." "We don't serve hamburgers, sir; try McDonald's." "Empty those garbage bins"; "we need napkins, Tom!" "How many Clam Chowders, lady?" "We're *not* out of Hush Puppies? How many, sir?" "Make that two Fish & Mores! . . . Working tomorrow, Cathy?" "See you; don't forget to punch out!"

It was eight-thirty. The stinging in my nostrils, my burning eyes, and aching feet found no relief when I stepped out into the heat through the back door facing the parking lot. I leaned on the door to remove my apron before heading for home. Home! The greasy air was a hand choking me, and now its grip was even tighter. What to do? The abyss was near. Rejected, discarded, just when I was doing well—I needed the Smiths. Just two more years and I'd be out on my own, in college. What would I tell them? What would I do? I'd heard of other sixteen-year-olds who got pregnant. Parents sent them away all hush-hush to some relative in Florida or to a home for unwed mothers. But I was a ward of the State! They'd send me there!

I walked across Halstad toward Glenwood Plaza. What if I told them I had been forcibly—?

I walked. The row of stores passed me on a conveyor belt. Would Carol believe me? I crossed another parking lot. *Run, why don't you run?* No sleep last night, so tired, tears burning inside, struggling to explode. *No, don't cry. Cross over to that street; keep walking.* My friend Lori lived near here; I couldn't tell her, she was a *nice* girl.

I quickened my pace. *Think, Crowell, think. Come up with a story, you've got to do it quick. If that jerk got you pregnant you've got to do something quick.*

Two girls were walking toward me on the sidewalk and as they approached, they noticed my dirty, perspiration-stained sailor's uniform and my apron dangling from the strap of my purse. I met the eyes of one and then the other. They turned their faces to each other and—laughed. Giggling, passing me, turning, staring. I broke into an unsteady run. Why couldn't I be like them?

Turn the corner, *think*, walk past these houses, cross that street, just like when you explored Beverly and came upon parks with grass like pillows, *think* now. More houses, curbed driveways, hedges, azaleas in pots along the walkways. *Stop and look both ways, Cathy, it'll be dark soon.*

Pick up that beer bottle lying at the curb; turn left here; ah, a park—swings, a slide! *Do you know what you have to do? You can do it, you* must *do it. She'll believe you. Don't cry; don't cry.*

It was dark now. I pushed my foot against the dirt to give me one last sweep forward on the swing. My shoe fell off. My left sock was rolled up around my toes. It was growing cooler; mosquitoes swarmed in the air, but I didn't pause to brush them away. The beer bottle was poking out of my purse. This would be a good place to do it. The park next to the Smiths' house was too dangerous. Someone could see me there. David and Mark and their friends were always hanging around that place; no, do it here. I'd walk home afterward along those houses on the other side by the trees and stay in the shadows. Just mess myself up a little—make it look good. It was the only way.

I was weak, shaking. My knees buckled as I made my way toward the trees on the other side of the park. I felt the tears coming, tears of anger and fear. Why did this have to happen to me? The back of my heel burned from rubbing against the shoe. I probably had gotten a blister from those stupid socks, but there were more important things to think about—I ducked into the trees and stumbled in an entanglement of brush, broken tree limbs, rocks. I couldn't see well enough to climb through them. Too dark.

I could hear running water somewhere in the darkness, so there was a stream nearby. A snarled tree stump tripped me and I fell on my hands in the mess of dead branches. Then I did cry. I had the beer bottle in my hand and I swung it around and hit myself. I hit my shin as hard as I could. I cried out in pain, I stumbled to the ground. Then I tore at the closure of my shirt, popping some of the buttons, leaving others hanging by threads.

Mosquitoes buzzed in my ears. I yanked at the front of my bra as hard as I could until it snapped. Fumbling, I ripped the buttons from my pants and tore the zipper to make it look as if they'd been forcibly removed. What if someone heard me? I crawled forward, inching toward the edge of the clearing. Nobody. Quiet. Street lamps lit the walk about one hundred feet away. I ran across the clearing, holding my clothes together with one hand and the bottle with the other.

It was getting late. Why was it taking so long? I was breathless, almost gasping. Wet with perspiration, I began scratching my stomach with the jagged edge of the bottle. I had to make it look good, but the *pain*. I hate pain. *Can't see what I'm doing, dark, the scratch stings, can't do this quickly.*

I made the marks where I thought was appropriate. Then I crossed my arms and pinched my chest and breasts as hard as I could, digging my nails into my skin. My hands were dirty and sweaty and I rubbed my tears from my face, leaving streaks of dirt. *Hurry, get this over with so you can get home. All you have to do is tie your apron around your front and no one will see a thing.* My hands trembled. I held my arms, pinching and squeezing as hard as I could. I bruised easily. I was shaking. Now pick up the purse with the crumpled apron. Begin to move along the uneven, weedy darkness to the light, the outer walkway. There were houses on the other side of the stoplight around the trees and at the corner. Walk in that direction, it's desolate.

I began to walk home, staying close to the bushes. Suddenly a light flashed on me. It startled me and I tried to duck behind a bush, but it was too late. It was the spotlight of a police car. I felt my entire body recoil. *Caught!* I was terrified. *Now* what was going to happen to me?

The policeman drew nearer, holding a flashlight. He called, "Police!" I couldn't think of what to do—run, duck—what story could I give? He would certainly see what I had done. "Let me see your identification," I said dumbly, trying to stall for time. *Come up with something, Crowell, some lie—something!* I couldn't say a thing.

"Are you all right?" the policeman asked. For a second I thought running would be my best option and I turned to take off, but found I was pinned with bushes on all sides of me. I cried harder. *I'm going back to the State this time for sure.*

I hated myself for crying. How could I have botched things up like this?

"Where do you live?"

For a minute I couldn't remember. Then I gave him my address.

"What's your name?"

"Cathy."

"Can you tell me what happened?"

I couldn't speak as myself, I couldn't think as myself. "I can't believe this is happening," I mumbled.

Another police car pulled up. I could hear the dispatcher's radio blasting voices. "I've got a rape victim here. . . ."

"I'm from the Glenwood Police Department. My name is Sergeant Shoeneck." I stared stupidly at him, trying to cover myself with my apron and purse.

"I think you'd better come with me to the station. Don't be afraid."

I held back, and for a brief moment I thought maybe I could tell him, "Thanks anyway. I'd rather walk."

"Nobody's going to hurt you. You're safe now," he said in a comforting tone of voice. "I'll take you to the Homewood Police Station and they'll fill out a report, and then your parents will come and pick you up." I was so embarrassed—what a humiliating experience.

"I know it's been a horrible experience for you, but we're here to help you. It's going to be all right now."

I remembered having this feeling before, this dread and alarm that I could never quite identify. I told myself to stop thinking.

During the drive I tried to gather my thoughts. I simply had to come up with some way to get out of this. *The police*, of all things. There would be reports to make out, attention, oh, this wasn't working out at all. What would I tell them? How could I possibly cover a rape story? *They'll know for sure I'm lying.* They were smart. They knew about these things. But I had no plan, no way out. I was thinking these things and babbling at the same time, so when we got to the station, Sergeant Shoeneck reported that I was a hysterical teenage rape victim. I froze, because now I'd have to face the law.

Sergeant Shoeneck coaxed me out of the car, telling me everything would be fine, not to worry, I'd be all right. His reassuring words made me feel terrible.

Nobody even had to ask what had happened. They all guessed and they all believed what I had just faked. I was taken into a room where I met a lady police officer named Anna Carroll. She seemed like a warm and sympathetic lady.

"Would you like a coat to cover yourself with? You're shivering."

I nodded and tried to hide my face. Why couldn't it have worked the way I had planned it?

"Would you like some water?"

"No. . . ."

"Do you want to tell me what happened?"

I blurted sentences which later I couldn't remember, words running together, falling out of my mouth, tearfully, almost as if I'd learned them somewhere else.

Officer Carroll wrote notes on her pad and asked me to describe, if I could, the person who raped me. I continued to whimper, wiping my face on the sleeve of the coat. I babbled on.

"Three men in a car? It's hard to follow you, I can't understand what you're saying—a white belt?"

It was a nightmare. This couldn't be happening.

Being caught in this lie meant I would have to come up with another, more elaborate lie to cover the first one. Like the complex stories I told Aunt Nellie. Adults were so scary and unpredictable. You always had to lie to them to get what you wanted, or to get them to like you.

I had seen enough movies to know that the police would wait a long time until they got a story out of a person. Eventually these police would insist I tell them a rape story. What if I told them right now that I wasn't raped, that I made it up? That would be getting caught in a lie! Never in all my life had I admitted I lied.

It wasn't long before Carol rushed into the room. Her face was ashen. "Cathy, oh, Cathy, honey. . . ." Carol ran to me and threw her arms around me. Just seeing her brought more tears, and then I was sobbing. If only she could save me from what was happening to me. Her eyes were large and pathetic. There were tears on her cheeks. She looked so concerned. Later I saw the expression on Bernie's face. It was as if something awful had happened to him personally. Even Officer Carroll looked upset.

Carol grasped my shoulders firmly and looked me in the eye. "Honey, is it true you were raped?" Her mouth was quivering.

What could I do? *They already believed*. I pressed my head against her and nodded yes. When I did that I felt something dark come over me, as though there were no going back.

Officer Carroll drove us to South Suburban Hospital in Hazelcrest to be examined by a doctor. I was certain he would discover I was lying. A doctor would know. My little scratches were only to impress the Smiths.

I heard Carol whispering to the nurse at the desk and I figured she was telling her I was a rape victim. I was taken into an examining room, where I had to take off my clothes and don a hospital gown. It was humiliating and I could feel my face turn red.

Carol was in the room along with Officer Carroll, the doctor, and a friend who had been playing cards with Bernie and Carol. Could it be any more embarrassing?

There I was, stripped and showing all those dumb bruises on my body, and they were all gaping at me as though I had really been hurt.

The doctor didn't say anything to me as he examined me and took notes. He drew a sketch of the scratchings on my abdomen, and I noticed Officer Carroll drawing one of her own at the same time. The doctor's face was cold and expressionless. He didn't make any gesture to indicate he believed I had been raped. I was sure he knew the truth.

Carol squeezed my hand hard and bit her lip. After the doctor took a vaginal smear and the nurse took pubic hair and a pubic combing, my examination was finished. The doctor asked me if I would like to have aspirins or a cold pack for my head. I told him no. That was when I was sure he was going to tell me right in front of everyone in the room that I most certainly had not been raped. But he didn't.

I left the hospital without so much as a Band-Aid on my body. The ride home in the car was quiet. A self-conscious, pained kind of silence rested on us, as if something terrible really had taken place. Well, it was all over now. I sank back into the seat, relieved and exhausted. That was the end of that.

It comforted me to know that this was one night I'd never have to relive.

14

July 10, 1977

I AWOKE AT about eleven o'clock the next morning. The Smiths were already assembled at the kitchen table having doughnuts and juice. The conversation stopped when I walked into the room. Mark and David fumbled and muttered, Carol was overly cheerful, Bernie was quiet and pensive, and the conversation never did pick up. They tried to act as if everything were normal.

As I was having my second doughnut, the thought struck me that Carol might tell someone about last night. *No. Don't take it seriously, Carol. Forget it now. It's over.* I felt the blood rush to my face. That's all I needed: people staring, friends not knowing what to say, boys giving me funny looks. I didn't want to have to talk about it again. I'd only have to make up more lies. *Carol, please don't tell everyone. It never really happened.* But I figured Mark and David had been told and that meant their friends would be told and that meant the whole school would be told and then—I lost interest in the doughnut.

"Why don't you and Lori do something together for a little while today?" Carol suggested. I shrugged; I had already thought of calling her. I'd let Carol think she was giving helpful advice. But it wasn't long after that when Lori was at the door. Had Carol already called her and told her everything? Why else would she show up practically the minute I woke up? I worried about that because I didn't want this lie to get complicated. I put on a pair of shorts and a pullover shirt and Lori and I rode our bikes up Ridge Road to the entrance of the Jewel-Osco Plaza. We parked our bikes to walk around and window-shop. I took her to a short row of stores just east of Long John Silver's, and since I figured she already knew about my lie, I said, "I got raped here last night."

"Huh?"

"Right over there," I pointed. "They grabbed me right over there." I was pointing vaguely toward the parking lot. Then I began to create the semblance of a story. It came spontaneously; one image followed another, and by the time I finished, here's about what I told Lori:

"A car went around that light pole over there, down that center part where they're building those buildings. They kept going around and around until they went around me. I tripped and fell and then these guys jumped out of the car and dragged me by my feet on the cold pavement to the car. There were two guys in the front and one in the back. The guy in the front held my legs and the guy in the back raped me, and then it was awful—I raked my fingers over his chest and face and ears. He bit me and cut me with a broken bottle."

I showed her the marks on my stomach and she paused, looked closer, and said, "But that looks just like little pin scratchings to me. Are you all right, Cathy?"

"Oh, sure." I wanted desperately to tell her what *really* happened and how, like a jerk, I stumbled right into the spotlight of a police car. *What would she say if I told her it was all a stupid lie? I made it up because I might be pregnant by this guy I know who lives in Beverly.*

I concluded the story. "They dumped me out of the car over by Glenwood Forest Preserve and they threw my clothes out after me."

She was speechless. "Well—I—they threw you out of the car? Are you all bruised?" She was smart. She had more sense than the police. They never asked me that.

"I mean, you bruise so easily, Cathy. You sure you're not hurt and don't know it?"

"Naw, they took me to the hospital and sent me home."

Lori shook her head. "One thing about you, Cathy —you certainly aren't emotional." And that was all we ever said about it. She never brought it up again. Then we went window-shopping, walking along the Plaza stores. I felt bad because I had lied to Lori.

That afternoon, Homewood police officer Anna Carroll paid a visit to the house. What did she want? Carol met her at the door and invited her in. Oh, how I wish she had told her politely, "There's nothing more to say. Cathy's said it all, the reports have been made; that's it." Oh, why didn't she say that? But Anna Carroll had come to ask more questions.

I babbled out a story with details, descriptions, and all the emotion I could muster. I wouldn't be dramatic, just emotional. *Give them what they want to hear. You want peril? I'll give you peril.* "And then, I felt myself being pushed out of the car and my clothes flew out after me —my shoes, my purse—"

"Oh, dear Lord!" Carol moaned. The lady officer wiped her eye with her finger and stopped writing. I was crying for real now. I cried because they had gotten what I thought they wanted from me and now I was trapped. They were satisfied. I felt sick.

Carol had never been so caring or attentive to me. But this was not how I wanted her affection. *Let the lie be over now,* I breathed. I wanted this to be the *last* time I'd have to tell the story. "I don't want to—have to tell this again—"

"Don't worry, honey, we're going to stand by you. The police are going to catch this guy, you'll see."

Now I was cooked. It was only a matter of time before my story would be blown to smithereens. I was stupid to think this would work in the first place. *No! They won't find the guy. There's no guy to catch.*

Officer Carroll stood up to leave. "We'll do our best, Cathy. You can count on that. We can't make any promises, but we've got a start, anyhow. This is a respectable family community here and we want to keep it that way. You can help us by coming down to the station and looking at some mug shots. . . ."

I knew it. Adults are shrewd. Here's where they would trap me. *Oh, no! I can't do that! I won't!*

Carol patted my knee. "Don't be afraid, honey. I'll be right there beside you."

I don't want to look at mug shots—I don't want to look!

Maybe there was still time to save myself without having to confess it was all a lie. I'd refuse to look at the mug shots. I'd tell them I couldn't face it. I'd say if I saw that horrible face again, I didn't think I could take it. No, there was no way I would ever go down to that police station to look at mug shots. *There was no face. There was no man.* Those policemen really knew how to ask questions to expose a liar. I must stay away from there, no matter what.

"No! I don't want to look!"

The women glanced knowingly at each other. "She's frightened . . ." Carol murmured. Oh, she cared! She really cared.

"I understand," the lady officer replied. "It's perfectly understandable. Maybe tomorrow or the next day would be better—"

I buried my face in my hands.

Did someone say, "You do want to see this guy behind bars, don't you?" as their voices became faraway and unreal.

Better lie and tell them yes, or they'll be suspicious. "Yes, I want him caught." *Keep up the performance.*

Carol walked the lady officer to the door and suggested Wednesday as a good day to go to the station. By then poor Cathy might feel a little better. She closed the door, leaned against the gold-tinted glass beside it, and observed her foster daughter sitting alone on the sofa.

The next days became a windstorm around me, pulling, yanking, steering me where I couldn't resist going. Everything had gone crazy. How could I stop now? Carol was so *loving* about everything. Monday, July 11, the gynecologist gave me an antibiotic injection and something to induce my period. I was once again exposed to peering eyes and stony faces and empty voices trying to give me assurance.

On Tuesday, July 12, I went to the Homewood Police Station. I sat on a chair while a thousand little faces trapped in books, all of them alike, looked out at me. *Not here. May I go home now?* But no, an artist with a sketch board entered the room. He coaxed me, "How's this chin? These eyes? Bigger? High cheekbones, you said, like this? And the hair was how long? Didn't you tell me collar length? Do you mean shoulder length? And what about a mustache? Did he have a mustache?" No, he *didn't*. "You're positive?"

My own voice flew over my head. I was sailing, lost. "I told you, *no mustache*. He was blond. You got that? *Blond*."

Another moment and the sketch became a face. Would this ever end? My fear of being found out compelled me to be graphic, detailed, emotional. "The eyes are bigger, I don't know about that mouth . . . the hair is stringier. . . ."

It would only be a matter of minutes now, hours maybe, before they confronted me with my lie. Carol would send me away. That would be the end of all this concern and caring. I was swept overboard; I had gone too far. She'd call me names—she'd hate me.

The policeman's voice was quiet and prodding. "Look again at this page."

"I want to go home. I want to go home now, please."

And I did. That night I stayed in my room with the door shut, trying not to think and trying to read. I was safe so far. No one had caught on yet. It was getting so complicated, though. It just kept getting worse, not better.

I don't know what time they showed up. It could have been noon or three or six or two—two officers at the front door. They were so *zealous*—didn't they have anything else to do? They gave me a handful of photos to look at. But I'd already seen enough! Carol was watching right along. She was "Mom" and Bernie was "Dad" and Mark and David were my brothers. A family always sticks together. I shuffled through the photos quickly. Handing them back, I said something like, "No, I don't recognize anyone."

"Are you sure? Look again."

I shivered. Felt the wind. I knew what they wanted— the photo that looked like the sketch. "Well, yes. . . ."

They were satisfied. It was as though a person had been created out of pencil lines and eraser marks. This couldn't be real.

And then the lineup. I had already identified the photograph of the blond-haired guy on the end—Number Two—now what could I do? They'd know I was lying if I didn't say anything. They'd *know* I wasn't telling the truth. I couldn't go home without pointing out the guy who looked exactly like the sketch the artist had made up. I pointed to Number Two. "That's him."

Of course he'd have an alibi. How could there be a conviction when there wasn't a rape? *Don't worry. Relax.* Why were these cops so eager to nail a guy? They didn't have anything to go on in this case, so why did I feel so pressured?

Be what they want. Do what they want you to do.

Officers Martin and Brandt told me there was someone else they wanted me to look at. They had already brought his picture to my house. "Do you recognize this one, too? He's a friend of the person you picked." *Look at this man again. Look at Number Five.*

Then the car. They wanted to know about the car. I couldn't remember what I had said. Did I say it was a

Nova? No, maybe an Oldsmobile. Now I was looking at pictures of cars. "Does this look like the car?" What could I tell them? I don't know much about cars. "Well, I think it was green. Or two-tone. Maybe it was a Cutlass. Nineteen seventy-five. I just can't be specific." I was running out of answers. My mind was going haywire, and I was running out of energy. I didn't know what to say the car looked like.

They'll know I'm lying if I don't come up with something. There was a picture of a Cutlass. "Could this be it?" I nodded. They were happy again.

Pressure. I wouldn't go any further. No, I wouldn't look at any more photos.

"I want to go home," I said. And so I went home. I went home and the blond-haired guy didn't.

He went to the Cook County Jail.

15

Chicago

I WAS NOTIFIED to appear at a pretrial hearing for the accused on Tuesday, August 16. I couldn't picture myself in a courtroom. I'd have to swear to tell the truth, the whole truth, and nothing but the truth, wouldn't I? The thought was horrifying, so I did the convenient thing for me: I didn't think about it. Every time the thought of facing the judge and telling my story came to mind, I quickly thought about something else. I couldn't tolerate the stomach-twisting nervousness and nail-biting, sleepless nights. I couldn't stand the thought of being found out. But my mind was so imprisoned that I saw nothing, recorded no details, and allowed myself no feelings during that brief hearing. I stood with knees and elbows locked tight, but my head was loose-hinged, wobbling with fatigue. I recited the words; they were recorded and sealed. I thought I heard tears but I wouldn't make sure. Someone's family members were crying, clinging to one another in the distance, and then there was the car again and me slouched in the corner, still undiscovered. I had known what to say and like a windup doll I performed the lie. I still felt not a twinge of guilt.

Fall 1977

I could tell there was something different about me. I could feel it inside, but I didn't question or look closely to see what it was. I didn't want to know about feelings unless they were those that I could understand and solve by myself. I didn't want to be confused, didn't want to ask questions of myself. Those questions would point to one answer I simply could not face. So for eight long years to come I would avoid self-introspection, avoid finding answers from inner resources that were not there. I avoided mirrors for a time and didn't give it a second thought. Nobody else seemed to notice anything different about me, so I dropped it from my mind. I laughed and gossiped, ate and slept, and I bought clothes to wear when Homewood-Flossmoor High School opened its giant doors for the fall semester to begin.

A goal began to form in my mind. It had begun when I was ten years old and still with Nellie, but it was only a kernel then. Now I could see the blossoming of that goal. It was no longer a dream, it was a reality I could achieve. My goal was to become independent and to take care of myself. Education, that was the key, I told myself. I'd get my education and support myself—then I wouldn't need anyone. This goal became a drive and an inspiration to me. It was a challenge, a pursuit. I could do it, I knew it; I was going to make my own way. I was going to take care of myself. I wasn't going to be anybody's ward or slave or tax deduction or artificial daughter or victim. I would be independent.

Having a plan like this was exhilarating. A coldness came over me that I liked and grew comfortable with. I could be self-reliant and less worried about being the odd member of the Smith family. Even the times when Carol showered my friend, Lori, with attention, ignoring me, I stopped feeling jealous. If Carol was angry at me and giving me the silent treatment, my stomach didn't churn anymore. Lori would come over and sit in the kitchen waiting for me while I got ready to go out with her, and Carol chatted happily and was warm and hospitable to my friend. But she'd give me the cold treatment. It would embarrass Lori and she would ask me, "Why does Carol do that? It makes me feel so weird."

I was desperate to make my own life. I put every opposition out of my mind. I would not let things get to me, no matter what. I would grit my teeth and stick it out until the day I could leave and be independent. I was developing scar tissue, calluses, on my heart. Nothing would stand in the way of my goal. I was going to get an education and I was going to get a good job.

Aunt Nellie took a turn for the worse. Her son moved her to Corpus Christi, Texas, to take care of her there, so I no longer had to make the trip to Beverly on weekends. Nellie agreed to let Carol and Bernie keep me, and it was only then my fear of the State began to fade. Gradually I began to see the advantages of my new surroundings.

I knew love was hard to get and I had only myself to hang on to, but I was safe for two more years, so maybe I could let down my guard just a crack. I had behaved indifferently when I arrived there, but being where there wasn't stress and fighting going on, I could almost allow myself the unfamiliar luxury of a good disposition. I began to think of myself as part of something "normal": a *normal* home, a *normal* family, *normal* responsibilities—a *normal* life. I wasn't restricted, grounded, or held captive in the backyard. There were no unfair, strict rules that were impossible to keep. No harsh demands, no sicknesses and smells of camphor. I was free to breathe at last.

After school I came home and worked on my homework at the kitchen table while Bernie cooked dinner. He made conversation with me. He asked about my homework, gave me his opinions, listened to me when I said something—*listened*. I didn't realize it, but I had never truly felt "listened to" before—not like this. Uncle Bill was a different kind of dad than Bernie. He showed his love by bringing home armloads of gifts for me, by playing and teasing and making jokes. He was the only man who ever loved me until Bernie.

Bernie talked and listened; he was gentle, warm, and I slowly started to believe I was there in his kitchen smelling his spaghetti sauce and writing my papers because he wanted me there. Never once did he imply I was lucky they took pity on me and let me in. Never once did he tell me how grateful I should be for his benevolence.

Boyfriends were never in short supply, and to my amazement, Carol and Bernie encouraged my dating and wanted me to date different boys so I didn't become too involved with just one relationship at such a young age. I wasn't as confined with Carol and Bernie and I wasn't unfairly restricted. But sometimes I didn't know what to expect from Carol. She was as moody as I was.

The weather was turning colder now. I wore winter clothing and walked across hard crusty lawns, and every day after school I rushed to the bus stop, my breath making clouds in the air, just to catch a glimpse of one person as he waited for the same bus.

He didn't look at me. I knew he saw me, knew he noticed, but he didn't look at me. It took me a couple of weeks of riding the same bus with him to realize he wasn't stuck up but shy. I was curious. What was his name? What grade was he in? Did he have a girlfriend? Would he ever talk to me? Where did he live?

By late fall of 1977 I could wait no longer for this handsome boy to talk to me. On a day that was gray and windy he carried books up to his eyebrows. When the bus ground to a halt at the curb, I jumped right in behind him, chirped a witty "Hi!" and when he took his seat by the window, the dark-haired girl who plunked down beside him was none other than me.

I introduced myself and found out all the information I needed to know about him: No, he didn't have a girlfriend.

He didn't ask me for a date, but he talked to me on the bus. Every day I rushed to the bus stop, hoping he'd be there. And he would be. Sometimes during the day

I'd catch myself thinking about him. I liked the feeling. I was impressed by his sweet disposition and his gentleness.

His name was David Webb and he was on the Homewood-Flossmoor gymnastics team. His specialty was the rings. I was lifeguarding for the school swimming pool and taking my advanced Water Safety Instructor courses after school. We had practice at the same time, so we took the same bus home.

It took David almost two months to ask me for a date. First we started walking together while I did all the talking, and then we'd meet at the bus stop, but our first official date was January 12, 1978. He came to pick me up at home and he was so handsome, standing there on the steps, his eyes looking directly into mine, a shy smile on his lips. I invited him inside while I got my coat. He was left to make conversation with Carol. That was a mistake.

He was awkward and his face was flushed when I joined him to leave, and later Carol told me he seemed unfriendly.

I'll always remember that first date because he was a perfect gentleman. It was quite a switch from the other guys I had dated. He brought me right home after the movie, said good night, and was gone. I wasn't sure I liked him more than anybody else, but I did lose ten pounds and got down to a size seven.

1978

1891–1978. Nellie Landers, beloved wife of James and mother of Charles and Francis, has gone to her heavenly rest. Internment and mass 9:00 A.M. October 5, Saint Barnabas Church, Beverly Hills, Illinois.

She died in Corpus Christi in a hospital. She had suffered a lot of pain in her final days, I was told. Her will included only her blood relatives.

Lying in the casket, she was wearing her favorite blue-

Top: In happier days—Cathy Crowell, age 2½, with brothers Steve, 10 (left), Don, 12 (right), and their mother, Georgia.

Above: Cathy at 3 years old with her Mickey Mouse birthday cake.

Right: At 6 years of age in Michigan, Cathy had not yet given up hope that her parents would come and get her and take her to her "real" home.

Left: Cathy's mother, Georgia Bourne Crowell: May 23, 1931–May 21, 1983.

Below: Nellie Landers (left) with Cathy and her mother (right).

Left: Cathy baked a cake for her eighth-grade graduation as Nellie Landers supervised.

Above: David Webb and Cathy Crowell on the way to her senior prom in 1979. The lie was just beginning.

Right: Cathy and her mother on Cathy and David's wedding day, July 11, 1981.

Below: David and Cathy's second child was born fifteen days after the death of Cathy's mother.

"I stand with Cathy in every way," said husband David. "We won't rest until Gary Dotson is granted a full pardon because he's innocent."

Left: The members of this little church gave Cathy comfort and support during the trying period following her recantation.

Right: Circuit Court Judge Richard Samuels, who originally sentenced Gary Dotson to prison, was the same judge who heard Cathy Webb's recantation at the April 1985 hearing. He upheld his conviction, and Dotson was returned to prison after one week of freedom.
PHOTO BY CHUCK BERMAN, © CHICAGO TRIBUNE, 1985.

Above: Rejoicing at Gary Dotson's release in April are his mother, Barbara (left), and his sister, Debbie (right).
UPI/BETTMANN NEWSPHOTOS.

Right: Cathy Webb leaves Markham County Courthouse after the hearing at which Judge Samuels sent Gary Dotson back to prison. "He's innocent!" she sobbed to the crowd outside the courthouse.
WIDE WORLD PHOTOS.

Above: At a press conference in Menomonee Falls, Wisconsin, Cathy discloses the results of the lie detector test. With her are attorneys Joseph Helm (left) and John McLario (right).

Below: At the May 1985 Illinois Prisoner Review Board clemency hearing, Cathy Webb and her attorney, John McLario, show the photo of Gary Dotson which closely resembled the sketch made by a police artist based on Cathy's false description of her rapist. The photo, however, was taken when Dotson was 17. He was 20 years old and wearing a full mustache at the time of his arrest.
UPI/BETTMANN NEWSPHOTOS.

Left: Warren Lupel, Gary Dotson's attorney, appeals to the Illinois Prisoner Review Board on behalf of his client.
© NEWS GROUP CHICAGO, INC., 1985. PHOTO BY RICH HEIN. WITH PERMISSION OF THE CHICAGO SUN-TIMES.

Above: At the clemency hearing, Illinois Governor James Thompson (left) refused to examine the false forensic evidence presented at Gary Dotson's 1979 trial. Cathy's attorney, John McLario, is on the right.

UPI/BETTMANN NEWSPHOTOS.

Right: Bernard Smith, Cathy's foster father, listens to testimony at the clemency hearing.

© NEWS GROUP CHICAGO, INC., 1985. PHOTO BY RICH HEIN. WITH PERMISSION OF THE CHICAGO SUN-TIMES.

Bottom Right: At the clemency hearing, Cathleen Crowell Webb's foster mother, Carol Smith, tells about the nail prints she saw on Cathy's chest the night of July 9, 1977.

© NEWS GROUP CHICAGO, INC., 1985. PHOTO BY TOM CRUZE. WITH PERMISSION OF THE CHICAGO SUN-TIMES.

Above: Cathy Webb and Gary Dotson at their first in-person meeting after the clemency hearing in May 1985.

Right: Author Marie Chapian with Cathy Webb in New Hampshire during the writing of this book.

and-white flowered dress. I had always thought it was
pretty, for an old-lady dress. I'm not sure what I saw
when I looked into the casket. She was so thin—for
Aunt Nellie, that is. So unlike her. Was she really dead?
I was afraid to look again. Her illnesses had emaciated
her and now, at this last moment, anyone who knew her
could gaze at her and she didn't even look like Nellie.
The people at the wake talked about a Nellie I didn't
know: a woman of energy, strength, courage, and a big
heart. They talked about her business mind and her love
for little children; about all of the wonderful things she
had done and the lives she had touched and the imprint
she had left on this world. I was amazed. Aunt Nellie
never told me any of this.

I sat in a straight-backed chair by the wall, looking at
the wreaths of flowers, and it occurred to me that some
of the people were sad. They felt a loss because she was
no longer among them. This, too, surprised me.

I had to sit through the wake and I felt nothing. Cold.
As I watched, people trickled in and later trickled out,
and I thought, *Who in the world is that?* I didn't know
she knew so many people. Then there was the funeral at
Saint Barnabas and the burial prayers. I had nothing to
worry about now because I wouldn't have to go back to
Beverly, and Aunt Nellie could never again tell me, "If
it weren't for me, you'd be in a State home."

My real mother called on Sunday nights. I answered the
phone that October night and her brown-sugar voice
came through the receiver. A blanket of tenderness
covered us.

"Ma! Aunt Nellie died." Now I could see her without
Aunt Nellie glowering over us as if we were truant brats
who crossed in between and not at the green. Mom
knew it, too.

"Sweetheart, we can be together more now." She
asked me if I still had that big bag of photographs of the
family. She wanted a certain picture.

"Ma, I'll have to dig them out for you. I stored them
in the basement."

When I talked to her later she could tell I was upset so she dropped the subject, but I couldn't. I had literally torn apart every corner of the basement, anywhere a bag of photographs might be. But they had thrown my family out.

My mother and I made plans for Friday night. I hopped into the living room to tell Carol and Bernie the good news. Carol's mouth drooped and you would have thought I told her I had wet the bed. Bernie stared straight ahead, eyes glued to the TV, bearing a patient smile. Carol, stone-faced, said only, "Oh." Nothing more than that.

But the meeting with my mother shouldn't have threatened Carol. It was embarrassing and awkward. When Mother's boyfriend's Chevy pulled up in the driveway with a tiny, dark-haired lady inside, I stared at her as if she were someone I had never met. Her boyfriend, a ruddy-faced man with a balding head, came into the house with her. He wanted to drop us off somewhere, but Carol wanted us to sit right in the kitchen. I guess we still needed supervision.

We sat at the table. Mother smoked her cigarettes and talked as the smoke came through her teeth with each word.

She smiled. Her teeth weren't as white anymore. They looked kind of yellow and crooked.

Mom had a job at Goldblatt's Department Store as a saleslady in the hosiery and shoe department. She didn't make much money, just minimum wage. She lived in a rented room in a woman's boarding house, run by a Greek landlady. Mother talked about her dream again, and it shocked me a little that she had clung to it all those years. She told it to me again, from the beginning. It had such significance to her!

"Oh, Cathy, we'll live in a nice little wooden house, not too fancy yet not shabby, by any means—and not too little either, you know? Just right. We'll have a dog, you'd like a dog, wouldn't you, honey? Your very own dog . . . and there'll be white ruffled curtains on the windows. . . ."

But I was getting older now. How could I tell her I was getting older?

When I closed the car door after her later, I ran into the house, not turning to wave good-bye. Inside the foyer I paused to remove my shoes and placed them on the little rug with the other shoes. Then in my room, with the door closed behind me, I sat on the edge of my bed and pulled from my pocket a tiny piece of paper with writing on it. I sat very still and for the first time in my life stared at my mother's address and phone number.

Was I imagining Carol's anger toward my mother? Was I too sensitive to stress? Surely I didn't imagine it when Carol said, "I'm jealous of her, you know. I always wanted a daughter." Sometimes I suspected Carol didn't want to give me the message when my mother called. That was when I remembered Nellie's glaring eye. Nellie, her huge dough arms barricading me from my brothers and my mother—and now Carol acting resentful about my relationship with my mother—was it happening again?

David and I continued dating, and that was another conflict because Carol didn't like David. Once again I was forced to sneak and lie; I lied about my work schedule at Service Merchandise Mart, I lied about where I was going and who I was going with, I lied about who that was I just talked to on the telephone. It became a way of life. If I was going to be accepted, I had to lie. I didn't want to lose my home and I couldn't openly defy Carol's wishes.

So I lied about a lot of things—about drugs, about getting drunk, about being where I shouldn't be. My David never got high. Never got drunk—at least not when he was with me. He was the perfect gentleman. And he loved me. When someone loves you, that means he is really important. I couldn't figure out why Carol didn't like David. He was such an all-American jock, and he was a *gentleman*. We didn't even start holding hands until we had known each other for two months.

And the first kiss he gave me was on the cheek, when he walked me to my Russian class in the *E* Building. Then he ran off.

The other guys I had dated were a girl's mother's dream because they knew how to charm the mother. But not David. What you saw was what you got. I liked that about him. I begged Bernie to invite David for dinner or to have him over just to watch TV. I'd sit there at the kitchen table and say, "Let's have David Webb over and we'll play UNO or some other game," because I thought they'd get to like him if they gave him a chance. I think they had him mixed up with someone else because in their minds he was a drunkard, a brawler, and didn't get along with his dad.

Carol didn't think I should go to the senior prom with David because Lori didn't have a date for the prom. "You should be ashamed to go and leave your best friend out," she told me at dinner.

"Cathy, can't you find a date for Lori, too? There's got to be *someone* who—" Lori shook her head, blushing. "Oh, I don't mind, Mrs. Smith. I'd feel bad if Cathy didn't go because of me."

When I fell in love with David I wanted to share my feelings with Carol and Bernie. I wanted to tell them how happy I was, but I had to lie about my happiness, and I guess that hurt most of all.

The envelope was dropped off and Carol put it on my dresser. I knew what it was. I passed it, pretending it wasn't there. It was the spring of 1979, prom time, the sweet smell of new grass coming up in the yards of Homewood, the great old oak trees along Ridge Road bending outward with limbs heavy in green buds, going without a winter coat; even Washington Square Shopping Center, with its concrete fields of parking lots and low, flat buildings, came alive with shoppers wearing pastels instead of winter browns and grays. I was in love, lilacs were about to bloom, all was well—except for one thing, one ominous, haunting terror—that white envelope on the dresser top in my room.

In two weeks' time, on May 22, 1979, I was ordered to appear in court. I had to point out a man and say he was guilty of a crime he hadn't committed. Why did I get into this mess? Why did I have to protect myself? Why couldn't I face the truth and tell the truth? Those are the questions I should have asked myself, but I didn't. Instead I asked, *How will I make them believe me?* What if they didn't believe me?

That's why I was nervous and that's why I couldn't open the white envelope until two days before the trial. It was the transcript of the hearing in 1977 and every word I said was right there. I *had* to read it. I read it, read it, read it—memorized it, like lines from a play. *I've got to make them believe me.*

"David, I have something to tell you," I said casually.

"Sure. What is it? A surprise?"

"Sort of. But not a good surprise."

"Not good? Carol is grounding you again, so you can't see me?"

"No, David. It's something else. I'm just going to tell you flat out, okay? In 1977 I was raped and now I have to go to court about it. The trial is the day after tomorrow."

David's face contorted. He sat that way for a long time, looking at his hands and cracking his knuckles.

"Don't say anything, David. I don't want to talk about it. Now I've told you and now you know, and let's just let that be enough."

"Court—you have to go to court?"

"I told you I don't want to talk about it."

"You don't want to tell me anything about it?"

"No."

And that was all we ever said about it. We never mentioned it again until after the trial when I told him the verdict and the sentence. I told him I didn't want to talk about it and he respected that. I couldn't elaborate that lie to him. I thought he would forget the whole thing, but many years later I discovered he hadn't forgotten at all.

May 21, 1979, at midnight, I was tossing around on my bed, looking at my pink room out of one eye because the other eye was buried with half my face in the pillow. The room was shadowy so it looked brown, blotched. *The guy's got to have an alibi. He's got to have witnesses. Nothing can happen. If they prove I'm lying, I'm sunk. I'll lose David. I'll lose everything.* Those prosecutors for the trial were so insistent: *Read the transcript of your testimony at the pretrial two years ago.* Well, I read it. I knew it by heart. *Let's see now, first they'll ask me to state my full name and spell my last name for the benefit of the court reporter. . . .*

16

Judge Richard Samuels' Courtroom
Cook County, Illinois
May 1979

A.   Cathleen May Crowell, C-R-O-W-E-L-L.

Q.   Miss Crowell, would you keep your voice up so that we can hear you, counsel can hear you? Miss Crowell, where do you reside? . . .

Cold, so cold in here. Wearing cotton, little black half-moons under my arms. Don't panic. Stay calm. Here it comes. Mrs. Hardiman looks like a mean one. There's a jury, look at them, do something to make them believe you.

Q.   Miss Crowell, I would like to direct your attention to July 9, 1977. That was a Saturday. Where were you living at that time? . . .

Let's see now, I punched out at about eight-thirty and at about a quarter to nine I went out the back employees' entrance toward the stores on my left. . . .

Q.   And did you, in fact, get off work about eight-thirty that evening?

A.   Yes, ma'am. Punched out at eight-thirty.

Q.   Did you have occasion to leave Long John Silver's? . . .

They'll ask embarrassing questions. That's what they told me. I don't mind that. I can handle it. Who was it who said they had the utmost confidence in me? Who said I would be a great witness? I can't disappoint them.

Q. Miss Crowell, what, if anything, of an unusual nature, did you observe in the parking lot at that time?

A. I noticed a car circling a light post to my right.

Q. Did you think anything about that at that time?

A. No, I didn't.

Q. Did you continue to walk?

A. Yes.

Q. And what, if anything, happened next, Miss Crowell?

What did that man tell me? I've got to be forceful.

A. I had passed a large commercial garbage can, looked to my right, and saw the car coming toward me. When it got close enough to me, I jumped out of the way and fell. . . .

Give details. Make it real.

A. They came toward me. One of them grabbed for my arm. The other one grabbed for my legs; my chest area. . . . They took me toward the car. The door was open, the back door, and I was put in feetfirst.

Q. After you were placed in the car, Miss Crowell, what, if anything, did these two men do?

A. One man went around to the front, the passenger side, and the other one got in the car right next to me. . . . He was about twenty years old or a little bit older than that. He had on a light-blue or white shirt, pullover, with buttons with piping. He had on blue jeans. He had on a white belt, he had long blond hair, about shoulder length. It was extremely greasy. I noticed his face, what it looked like, his mannerisms.

Q. When he got into the backseat with you, Miss Crowell, how close did he come to you at that time?

A. He was about a foot away from me, face to face.

But don't ask what he looks like. All these descriptions! It's too much.

Q. And what position were you in at that time after being put into the backseat?

A. I was laying on my back faceup with my legs bent.

Q. And what position did this man in the backseat take?

MR. FOXGROVER: Objection. It is suggestive —talking about a position of some sort. There's nothing in evidence that he was in the car.

THE COURT: Mr. Foxgrover, are you not in a sitting position at this moment?

MR. FOXGROVER: Yes, I am, Your Honor.

THE COURT: The word *position* does not seem to me to be suggestive.

MR. FOXGROVER: There is no evidence he was in the car, with all due respect.

MRS. HARDIMAN: With all due respect, Your Honor, she testified he got into the backseat with her.

THE COURT: Such was the testimony. Please proceed. . . .

Q. (Continuing by Mrs. Hardiman.) What exactly was he doing?

A. Held [me] down with his arms putting his weight on me and I was trying to get away from him.

Q. Miss Crowell, what happened next?

A. The car started up. They took—they left on the service road up toward Ridge Road. They went up the service road and at that time when they were turning, the man in the backseat tried to turn me. . . . I ended up with my head on the passenger side; my head between the seat and armrest and my legs were on the driver's side. . . .

They're going to go over the whole story. They're going to ask me everything. Give details. Make it real.

Q. When you say "he," Miss Crowell, to whom do you refer?

Point at him. Be effective.

A. To the defendant. This man.

Q. Let the record show the witness has identified the defendant in this matter. . . .

Swimming. I'm swimming. Hot. How long is this going on?

A. . . . He used the beer bottle to write something on my stomach. It must have been some kind of a
joke. . . .

Q. What were the other two occupants doing at this
time?

A. They were talking to the defendant about what
he was writing and what he should write.

*What if they ask me what they were suggesting he
write? What will I say?*

Q. What happened after the writing on your stomach?

A. He was still trying—still kissing me. . . .

*Now what? Where did I tell them he pulled over?
Where was that?*

Q. Did you know where the car pulled over at that
time?

A. No. I knew it was on the side of a road. I just
heard the gravel.

Q. What happened after the car pulled over?

A. I was pushed out of the car. . . . (*Gravel! I said
gravel. There's no gravel there! I didn't have any gravel
marks on me, either!*)

Q. Did you ever give the police a description of that
vehicle?

*I don't remember what I told them. Oh, no. Did I tell
the police? Did I tell the lady at the police station? I
don't know much about cars.*

A. Yes, I did.

Q. What color was that vehicle?

A. I am not sure. It could have been light-colored
on the bottom. It was a darker-colored top. It was a
four-door. . . .

*Give details. If you give details, you can't look like
you're lying.*

. . . there was a tear on the upper deck on the rear of
the car. I had torn it a little when I was struggling. There
was an armrest in the front seat. There was a reflector
above the rearview mirror. . . .

Q. You described that reflector as three inches,
didn't you?

A. Yes.

Q. Did you make any other precise description of that vehicle, Miss Crowell?

A. There were no seat belts hanging from the roof of the vehicle. There were small headrests. The driver's side headrest was lifted up off the seat. There was beer in the backseat on the driver's side. There was no hump in the backseat.

Q. So, even though this rotten event was going down, you did have an opportunity to make specific observations, isn't that correct?

He's on to me. This is it. Now they've got me.

A. Yes, I did, sir.

Waiting. *How long do we have to wait?* It was the end of a three-day trial. We sat drinking Cokes, Carol and Bernie trying to be pleasant. At least I was getting their attention. The lawyer had asked how close I was to the defendant's face and I told him I was close to his face the entire time. I said, *At times he never went away from my face.* But then I said I couldn't see the color of his eyes. I knew they'd catch me on that one. And then I said the vivid details of that automobile were "permanently etched in my mind." That was stupid. What if they made me come forward and look at his face? I could never look at him. Never. I could never go through with it if I looked at him.

We were filing into the courtroom. It was so big, so scary. I never wanted to see another courtroom. *I just know he'll be found innocent. Everything will be fine as long as they don't question me again.* I hated it when they questioned me. I couldn't remember which lie I had just told.

There is a picture in my mind, and it will be there for the rest of my life. It's a picture of a young man: his shoulders are shaking and he's sobbing after the verdict is read.

We went out to eat then. I think I ordered a cheeseburger, french fries, and a Coke. We didn't say much, but Carol looked relieved. Johnny Cash was singing "I Walk the Line" on a jukebox and outside the window it looked as if a wind was stirring up. Newspapers were blowing on the sidewalks; people were walking with their heads down. *Well, Cathy, you've certainly done your duty. You've proved that justice always prevails.* I looked out the window and continued eating in silence.

What must that man be thinking now? He knows and I know that he didn't do it. Outside the window people continued to walk with their heads against he wind. I would finish my cheeseburger and walk with them.

"We can't leave until you have some dessert, Cath," Carol said brightly. "They have German chocolate cake, your favorite!"

I sighed. "Yeah, I'll have cake."

Back home, I went directly to my room, where I intended to spend the whole night. I had a romance novel I wanted to start, but I couldn't concentrate. I thought I saw the pink walls moving. My imagination and my jangled nerves wouldn't allow me to read. I closed the book and joined the family in the living room to watch TV. Then I remembered I had to call David.

"Well? How'd it go?"

"How'd *what* go?" I answered.

"You know, the trial."

"Oh, that. Okay, I guess. Did you watch 'Real People' tonight?"

"What was the verdict?"

"Oh—guilty, I guess."

David was silent. Maybe I'd try to sneak away tomorrow and see him. I was sneaking away more and more. Often I'd tell Carol and Bernie I was going to visit my friend Nancy at the University of Illinois, but I'd go see Liz. (She was also a student at the University of Illinois.) It created more tension for me than I wanted to try to handle. Tension, nothing but tension.

David couldn't write to me at home because Carol would read the letters. So we took out a post office box, and I received my letters from him there. His sister would bring me letters from him, too.

The verdict was guilty.

I had to remember an incredible number of interlocking stories. It got so confusing—where David was concerned, where my mother was concerned. I thought it drove Carol wild when I talked to or saw my mother. When I turned eighteen, Carol and Bernie let me drive, and I bought my own car for fifteen hundred dollars of my savings. So now I could pick up my mother anytime I wanted to.

On July 12 I was outside in the backyard, idly watching construction workers hauling lumber up the driveway for the construction of a new two-car garage, when Carol emerged from the house. "Well, he's been sentenced," she announced.

"Huh?"

"The rapist. He got twenty-five to fifty years."

Oh, my God! I didn't flinch. "Really?"

"He's in jail now. So you don't have to worry about a thing."

Nausea swept over me. *Stay calm. Don't say anything. It's going to be all right. He'll appeal. He'll get out. Something will turn up. I won't worry about it. I won't think about it. I won't.*

Aquilla Park
July 27, 1985

We are walking through the trees and Cathy is pointing out the area she came to the night of July 9, 1977. It was here she ducked into the trees to cut herself and tear her clothes, she says, and it was here she began fabricating her lie.

"Cathy, you knew that a man had been arrested because you identified him in a lineup. What did you do when you left the police station that night?"

"I just went home, that's all."

"But Cathy, a man was in jail and he was innocent. Didn't you think about that?"

"I forced myself not to. I told myself that he would never be convicted because he'd have an alibi. All I cared about was that I hadn't been caught lying. That was the most important thing to me."

"So Gary Dotson was just an object. He wasn't really a human being. He stood there in the lineup as a *thing*, and you pointed out something that you really weren't aware was a real person."

"You know, Marie, you're right. It was years after that day in the police station before I thought of him as a person with a *name*."

"And at the pretrial hearing? Before a Grand Jury judge, did you see Gary Dotson sitting there, and did you look at his face?"

"Of course not. At the trial the defense attorney asked me to move closer to the accused. I remember a flood of terror came over me because I could *never* look him straight in the eye. That would have killed me. So they took my reactions to mean that I couldn't stand to be close to the man who had attacked me."

We're walking in the grass and we can hear the traffic on 187th Street. Bells ring in Glenwood School across the street and I ask, "Did they ring that night?" She tells me no, they didn't. "At the pretrial, you virtually stood next to Gary Dotson, Cathy, facing a judge. Do you remember that?"

"Vaguely. I don't really remember Dotson."

Cathy looks at me with unclouded eyes. I can tell that this is not the same girl who faced the judge that day. She has a conscience now and she's deeply stirred. "You see, I have just a vague recollection of going before that judge. I barely remember the pretrial hearing. I was trying to forget it even as it was taking place. Bits and pieces come to my mind, but I can't remember clearly. What I do remember is what I did to myself right here in this park."

I look into the trees and see the snaggled, snarled mess of weeds and tree stumps, rocks, and briars. This is where she fell and this is where she tore her clothes. She's looking around and trying to retrace her steps.

"You see, I never *imagined* being raped. I always knew it was a lie, a fabrication. All during the pretrial hearing and the trial itself in 1979, it was the *lie* I concentrated on. I simply couldn't be discovered. I would do anything to keep that lie alive."

"Could you tell the lie from the truth?"

"Yes, I knew I was lying. I didn't lie as some kind of wish fulfillment. My world was a 'now' world and my main goals and thoughts were to gain what I wanted. The only way I could get what I wanted was to take it any way I could. I accomplished that by lying."

South Chicago
On the Dan Ryan Expressway

Cathy and I are driving from Homewood to Beverly Hills in a rented Chevette which has been jerking and stalling since morning. The windows are rolled down and the hot wind, choked with freeway fumes, blows through the car. Cathy's at the wheel and her hair is blown straight up into a peak, like whipped cream. We can hardly hear ourselves over the sound of the crowded lanes of engines, exhaust pipes, and tires, so we're shouting at each other.

"If this were nine years ago, Cathy, and you were fifteen years old, how would you feel, sitting here like this?"

"I'd probably think about other things—I'd get my mind off what was happening."

She tries the starter again, the engine gives a tired groan, and we jerk forward. We're laughing now, relieved. "Cathy, tell me about the kinds of things that upset you when you were fifteen years old."

"Carol not talking to me, going back to Nellie's on weekends. . . ."

We turn off the freeway to her old neighborhood. She stops to point out something. "There's the library where Liz and I used to hang out. We're on One hundred eleventh Street and you can see it's one of the largest hills in town. Nellie didn't want me coming over here or riding my bike on this hill, so naturally I did it all the time." She laughs. "We sat right there in the grass and read everything from *The Chronicles of Narnia* to romance books."

"Romance books?" Suddenly I'm alert. "Tell me about that. What did you read?"

On August 16, 1977, at the pretrial hearing, Cathy's rape story was believable. In 1979, her testimony in the Markham County courtroom convinced the twelve men and women on the jury, and after a ninety-six-minute

deliberation (including lunch) it was unanimously concluded that Gary Dotson was guilty of aggravated kidnapping and rape. When Cathy came forward in March
1985 to confess that her testimony had been a lie and
Gary Dotson was innocent, those involved in the earlier
court decision, as well as her foster parents and the
police who picked her up the night of the incident, were
stunned by her confession. How could they have been
duped—conned by a sixteen-year-old?

Studies show that the more vulnerable and virtuous a
woman appears in a rape case, the more credible her
story in court. Cathy fit this description as a sixteen-
year-old who was erroneously described as a virgin by
the prosecutor. Gary Dotson, on the other hand, appeared less virtuous. He had a police record for petty
thievery, truancy, drunken behavior, and disorderly
conduct. Cathy was a good student at Homewood-
Flossmoor High School and Gary was a high school
dropout who had been truant forty-six days during his
last year in school. He looked disreputable at the trial
while Cathy looked, as one person said, "like apple pie,
like the figure on top of a wedding cake."

How could a young girl fabricate such an elaborate lie
that hoodwinked intelligent, serious adults?

The clue that was missed in all the proceedings of this
case centers on Cathy herself. If the story was a lie,
where did she get the idea to tell such a story? In the
days I spent interviewing Cathy, I searched for an
answer to this question.

The answer was almost comically simple. Her story
came from the stories she read. She got them from the
library, from friends, even Carol brought romance
novels home by the grocery bag full. (They were given to
her by her mother.) I asked Cathy for the names of
some of them and read them all.

Cathy's fictional rape creation was practically lifted
from the pages of books like *Sweet Savage Love*, by
Rosemary Rogers, a book that she was reading at about
that time. It contains a violent rape of the heroine by
three drunken men.

This book, like the rest of the genre, is sado-
masochistic in theme. The reader's senses are numbed
and dulled by these stories of brutality and rape. By the
time she has finished the book, the reader is desensitized.

Cathy didn't fantasize herself as one of the romance
story heroines—she was desensitized to it. She wasn't
fulfilling a fantasy when she concocted the rape story,
she was acting on the familiar—much as a child plays
cops and robbers after watching several hours of cops
and robbers on TV.

Cathy said she scratched, like the victims in the
books. She described under oath in 1979 how she
scratched and the assailant laughed.

Q. Where did you scratch him?
A. On his chest.
Q. And what happened after you scratched him?
A. He sat back and laughed.

> . . . *she sought to scratch or claw him anywhere she
> could but always a hand or elbow was there to stem
> her effort. He laughed as if enjoying her struggles
> . . . she became like a wild thing . . . biting, clawing
> at him. Yet he only laughed. . . .*

Cathy said she scratched her "attacker" behind his
ears and on his chest. Yet when Gary Dotson was picked
up by the police on July 15, there wasn't a trace on his
body showing he'd been scratched.

Cathy described being *bitten* by her attacker. (On her
body, however, were only fingernail prints made by her
own fingers.)

> *Then as viciously as if he were a mad dog, he
> sank his teeth into her shoulder.*

There are literally hundreds of accounts of biting by
cruel attackers in those books that Cathy read.

Another injury Cathy performed on herself was to
scratch her abdomen with a sharp piece of glass. Why

not? The heroines in the books are cut up every day
—and so are the men. Knives are favorite weapons of
women and a conventional weapon in all these stories.

> *Before Paco could move a muscle, Ginny had used
> her knife to scratch a thin, oozing line across Con-
> cepcion's heaving belly.*

It isn't surprising that Cathy would naturally assume
she needed to have a few cuts in addition to the bruises
on her body to make it look as though the deed had been
a violent one. *Helter Skelter* was a popular book and
movie at about that time, with its images of carved-up
victims.

Cathy didn't know that in *real* life a violent rapist
does more than leave little pin scratches and fingernail
marks on his victims.

Cathy made certain to tear her clothing, something
essential to every rape scene in the novels. It's rare in
these romance books that a woman willingly disrobes.
Often, she is left a pitiful figure in the aftermath of
violence, clinging to her tattered clothes.

If Cathy had read real-life accounts of rape, she'd
have known the grim reality was different from what
she read in the romance novels. She would have known
that the fictitious characters are ridiculous parodies of
human beings and an embarrassment to both sexes.

How does a sixteen-year-old assimilate such information from these books? Add the sex education the media
provides and a lifetime of lovelessness. How realistic
would this sixteen-year-old girl's evaluation be—especially a child who had the emotional deficits that
Cathy had?

There are four necessary building blocks a parent
gives a child in order for him to grow with a basis of
well-being; they are: a sense of belonging, a sense of
worth, a sense of safety, a sense of competence. When
any one of these is missing, the child does not develop
an awareness of being acceptable or "okay."

Why did Cathy read these romance books? She was

interested in the clothes and culture of the sixteenth through the nineteenth centuries, and often read history books on the same subject. Subconsciously her mind stored details from these romance stories, and she later saw rape as the perfect cover story to exonerate her promiscuity and possible pregnancy.

Cathy's performance was scripted well. Now the catch: she only wanted it to *appear* to her foster parents she had been raped. Her little drama had been staged for a private audience only. She had no intention of allowing the public in. The Homewood Police crashed the show. The tears of frustration, anger, and fear at being discovered were what Officer Schoeneck and Anna Carroll witnessed. Once Cathy began creating her tale of rape, giving details and reciting scenes she had once read about, she couldn't stop. She wove her web and she saw no way out.

Let me be clear, I am not saying that these sort of books produce false accusations of rape. But for someone who was confused, and emotionally distraught, these books provided the script for the lie she had decided to tell.

There is another issue worth pointing out. Cathy never manifested the aftereffects of a rape victim. The real rape victim experiences many disrupting emotions: nightmares, self-blame, anger, fear of physical violence, depression, suicidal thoughts, feelings of uncleanness, confusion, helplessness, paranoia, extreme nervousness and agitation, and fear of men. Sometimes these symptoms take weeks, even years, to work out. Cathy didn't display these overt responses. She didn't have nightmares, phobic reactions, or disturbed patterns of eating and sleeping. She had no irrational fears of objects associated with the traumatic experience: cars, lonely roads, parking lots, or shopping malls.

Phobic reactions, which some victims develop as defense mechanisms, were not present in Cathy then, nor are they now. Phobias don't just go away by themselves so chances are, if Cathy developed a phobia then she'd still have it today. But she's not afraid of New

Hampshire's dark roads, its parks, its shopping malls, or that a rapist is lurking outside her door.

Perhaps most significant, she continued dating and after meeting David, she eventually began going steady with him. She was not afraid of men.

Also important, Cathy did not engage in one of the most common responses of the rape victim: irrational self-blame, the "If only I had done something differently!" feeling.

Cathy's guilt feelings were minimal. She was a victim of *fear*, not guilt. When her foster mother overheard Cathy crying in her bedroom, it was not Cathy's real feelings she related to but ones she imagined.

Carol also told her words to this effect: "Don't worry, you're not going to have to be an old maid just because you're not a virgin anymore. Some man will want you, you'll see. It won't make any difference to him at all." These words only confirmed to Cathy the need to lie because she had been sexually promiscuous for so long.

She had not engaged in acts of sex unwillingly. The reason she could lie and behave promiscuously was that her moral system was built on the infantile belief that sin and lying were only bad if one was caught and punished. That is why, even when her fear of pregnancy was dismissed, she continued to support the lie. She couldn't risk being found out. She was compelled to defend her lie or be assaulted by guilt. If she could remain undiscovered, she would feel guiltless and of course there would be no punishment—no withholding of love or "being sent back to the State." Cathy's fear of rejection and punishment was more real to her than an awareness of what was morally right.

Cathy didn't digress academically, a significant point. In fact, she did well in school, which resumed less than a month after the brief pretrial hearing on August 16, when she and Gary Dotson stood before the bench. She made friends at school, was popular with boys (although some boys threw furtive glances her way and talked among themselves from a distance when they heard she had been raped), and, except for the momentary reminders in court of the lie she had told, her life appeared normal. She didn't think about the twenty-year-old innocent man, Gary Dotson—she didn't think of *him* at all.

She did not see someone with a mother, a brother, and four sisters, who lived in a house similar to the one she lived in, who loved to climb trees as a kid, who ate pizza and popcorn and tied his shoes, brushed his teeth, bled when he was cut, cried when he was without hope. . . .

She saw no one.

17

Homewood
1978-1979

I TAUGHT SUNDAY school at Saint Joseph's with Lori. We shared the first-grade class. I taught the basics of the Catholic faith: the Apostles' Creed, the Our Father, and the Hail Mary. The children looked up at me with their open faces and clear, bright eyes and I would fill them with admonitions such as, "Remember now, God expects you to be *good*."

How on earth could a person be good enough to please God? Maybe if I did well in school I could please Him. I seemed to fail at everything else. The children in my CCD classes were like little birds with their beaks open. They swallowed whatever we fed them. I had been like that once. I believed if I just said enough penance prayers God would be satisfied. I don't know when I stopped believing that, but I did. Somewhere along the line I lost my interest in God. I had to find another meaning for my life.

That was when I made studying and school even more important to me than ever. It meant more for me to do well in school, get good grades, achieve, and prove myself, than almost anything else. I was determined to make my own way, and to make the name *Crowell* mean something. My name was really all I had of my family, so I wanted to make it a name that people would sit up and notice. I received an award in my senior year. It was from the Illinois State Scholarship Commission—a certificate of merit in recognition of Outstanding Performance for the 1979–1980 State Scholarship Competition. I received this Illinois Scholar's Award on a parchment-paper certificate signed by Governor James Thompson himself. I looked at my name on the award many times and each time I thought to myself, *This is only the beginning.* When I showed the award to Carol, however, she ignored it.

I knew my brother Steve lived somewhere in New Hampshire. My mother gave me his phone number and I excitedly gave him a call. I needed something of my roots, something—I didn't know what. It was almost more than I could believe to hear his voice on the other end of the phone—a man's voice. My brother Steve was a grown man! Twenty-five years old. I still saw him in his sneakers and blue jeans, grinning at me from the branch on the cherry tree back at Aunt Nellie's. He invited me to come up and visit him in New Hampshire, so I took a two-week vacation. But before I arrived, he was in a bad car accident and had to be hospitalized. His wife, Leslie, told me he was lucky to be alive. The day I showed up was the day he was released from the hospital. He wasn't feeling well and was in a cranky mood because of the pain and discomfort he felt. But I didn't mind because this handsome man was my brother!

Steve was a businessman; he owned a steel construction company and was very successful. I was amazed to see what this brother of mine had built. He had been a wild kid, I was told, but now look at him! I discovered how alike we are because he is the kind of person who hides his feelings to protect himself, too. Sometimes I would wonder what he was thinking. He was intense and intelligent; he could be loving and sweet one minute and then bite your head off the next. I was

amazed to realize that there was another person in this
world whose blood was the same as mine, and who was
in some ways like me. I wanted to feel immediately close
to him, but that feeling didn't develop.

I was taken by the beauty of the country, the peace
and quiet of New England. I felt relief from the tension
at Carol and Bernie's. Steve, his wife, Leslie, and their
two children showed me that I did belong to a family,
that it wasn't just a dream, and that this family could be
normal, just like all the other families in the world.

After graduation from high school I attended Prairie
State Junior College. I had wanted to attend a state
university, but Carol and Bernie couldn't help me with
the federal grant applications, and I had no idea where
my father was. Things at home were becoming so
uncomfortable because of my sneaking and lying to see
David and the conflict with Carol over my mother, that
I began to feel the world closing in on me. I wanted to
cry or scream or stamp my feet, but I did none of
those things. David was practically the only one who
could draw me into a calm, happy state. My mother was
second.

Things weren't normal in Homewood. I didn't belong
to the Smiths. I wanted to be on my own. I knew that
Bernie understood my feelings because he had lived in
another home for a while when he was a boy. But now I
felt that my conflict with Carol over my mother and
David were more than I could take. After a confronta-
tion with Carol over not being able to see my mother on
Mother's Day, I felt I had to get away. I made plans to
go to New Hampshire, carefully sneaking things out of
my room in garbage bags, a little at a time. I even left a
short note in the drawer of my nightstand, telling them I
loved them but asking them not to try to find me.

David wouldn't let me go alone. He insisted he'd
come along. I really wanted to be by myself, to get my
thoughts collected, but he worried about my going
alone, so in May of 1980 David and I drove away in my
Buick Regal for New Hampshire. We stayed with my
brother Steve, who welcomed us warmly. He realized

David was going to be with me and they became friends. After we had been there only a couple of days, David said, "Your brother is really a terrific guy." It was so easy for him! He just allowed himself to feel good feelings. That was the big difference between David and me. He could have trust and genuine love for people without any problem. He believed all people are basically good.

We found a little place of our own in Antrim, a village of two thousand people about twenty minutes from Steve's house. Antrim is a little town nestled on a hillside sloping toward the Contoocook River. Many of the buildings go back to 1777, when the town was incorporated. To the west were the Uncanoonuc Mountains, and at certain spots you could catch a clear view across the Merrimack Valley. We lived in an apartment in a huge old white wooden house with green shutters and fenced porches. It had pillars and trellises, flowers and manicured grounds. It was like a dream cottage set on a quiet winding street next to other white wooden houses with shutters. I thought we would be happy.

But David began working for my brother, erecting steel beams and columns at building construction sites all over New England, and he left for work between four-thirty and five-thirty in the morning and didn't get back until seven-thirty at night. He worked outside in the sun all day, so by the time he sat down to dinner with me, he could hardly keep his head up. I sat there, all ready to talk and have a nice evening, while he fell asleep in his food. Things weren't the way they should be. Deceiving David's parents made us feel terrible— we were living together. I didn't want to lie to them— anyone but them.

My mail was being forwarded from a post office box in Chicago. Carol found out the box number and sent me several letters, expressing her hurt feelings over my leaving home. I wrote back after the first letter, trying to explain my feelings. But when David realized she didn't respond to my letter in a positive way, he insisted that I leave the other letters unopened. We did not make

contact with Carol and Bernie again until just before
our wedding.

I sat around during the days with nothing to do. I ate
cookies, slept, ate potato chips, read (no more romance
books—they weren't available). I was unhappy. I
wanted to go back to Chicago. I was going through
culture shock. I took walks along the narrow streets of
Antrim, up and down the sloping hills. In the distance I
could see the mountains, quiet, still. There was nothing
to get upset about. The only friction was the buzzing of
a bee along the side of a barn. Old buildings were never
torn down in New England. Everything stayed old. If a
barn was collapsing, it was allowed to slowly fall. No
shopping malls, no fancy theaters, no Long John
Silver's—my breath caught in my throat. *Why did I say
that?*

By the time I was back in the apartment I was
sweating and trembling. I had left school without taking
my calculus final. I had unfinished business. I *had* to
finish things. That's why I *had* to finish the lie. I
couldn't just drop it without completing it. It had to
have a conclusion. *Stop thinking.*

I went to the kitchen and began pulling food out of
the refrigerator. I fixed a hamburger casserole for dinner and baked biscuits. School. What about school? I
had wanted to *be* someone. I still did. I had worked
hard in high school. I *had* to go back and finish college.

Why did I say Long John Silver's? But it was too late
to hide the picture of that weeping, innocent man.

Steve noticed how unhappy I was and figured it was
because I was bored. He gave me a job in his company
as a bookkeeper and at Christmastime I had finally convinced David, by a constant flow of tears and begging,
that we should go back to Chicago for the holidays.
With both of us working we had saved enough money
for the trip. But even there, things didn't really change.
I was still agitated, nervous, upset. I tried to hide my
feelings and put up a good front, but I was irritable and
short with people. That was the only sign I ever gave of
the discontent I felt inside. Carol was angry with me for

running away and wasn't speaking to me, so we stayed with David's folks. The best thing about that Christmas was the engagement ring I received from David.

1981

We set our wedding date for July 11. The marriage was to take place in Homewood at Saint Joseph's Catholic Church. David's parents wanted to have the reception in their home. They were already hard at work making the preparations. David and I were scheduled to start attending the prenuptial classes in a Catholic church in Keene, New Hampshire.

In January of 1981 I decided I should work where there was more diversity, so I took a job at Brookstone, a mail-order company outside Antrim, as an inventory control clerk. I complained about the prenuptial classes to a girl whom I was training to be my assistant at work; she was a warm, friendly girl named Kathy. She wore her blond hair parted in the middle and curled under at the shoulders. I had noticed that she always wore a dress to work and not slacks, as the rest of the girls did. She had a scrubbed and wholesome look about her. I enjoyed talking with her because I hardly knew anyone in New England, and I needed a friend.

"I don't know why we have to take these prenuptial classes," I complained.

Kathy chuckled. She told me she went to a Baptist church. "Guess they want to make sure you're serious about marrying this guy," she said.

"You can't believe what we have to go through to get married. I have to produce our baptismal and confirmation certificates, my parochial school records, and they want to be sure we're practicing Catholics. Now, how do we prove that?"

"By your church attendance, I suppose."

"On Sundays we sleep."

It felt good to have someone to talk with. After a

pause I asked, "Tell me, what do Baptists believe?"

"We believe in what the Bible says. Have you ever read the Bible?"

The Bible. I had seen only two in my life: one on the table at mass at Saint Barnabas and one in Nellie's attic. "That's the book Moses wrote filled with stories on how to live a good life," I answered. "I'd like to read it sometime."

Kathy looked at me with a studied expression, as if she couldn't decide whether I was kidding or not. Then she smiled. "Are you interested in learning what the Bible says?"

"Sure. I've always been fascinated by it but I've just never really had the opportunity to sit down and read it."

She invited me to a Bible study in Peterborough and I accepted. Why not? David was working out of town most of the time and I'd be alone in the apartment anyway. What could it hurt?

I was tired and unhappy most of the time. Nothing seemed satisfying. David and I talked about our "living in sin" and decided maybe that was the reason for my misery. After all, I wanted our relationship to be perfect. Maybe we should live separately until after the wedding. I wanted to be independent but I couldn't part with him. It was so confusing, so depressing.

We had to attend the prenuptial classes in order to be married in the Catholic church. We drove to Keene, a city of about twenty thousand. We took our places in the class with two other couples. We were tired and so were the other couples. Nobody talked or smiled. The nun who was teaching explained that marriage isn't all love and romance, that there are financial obligations, too. (David fell asleep at that class and I daydreamed about our married life and living in a wooden house, not too little and not too big, with polished floors and white ruffled curtains on the windows . . . and a dog. . . .)

18

Antrim and Chicago
1981

IN FEBRUARY OF 1981 my brother Steve called me. He was quite upset. "Mom's really sick, Cathy. We'd better fly back to Illinois. I'll pay for your plane ticket. Get ready right away."

I thought my heart stopped beating. "How sick is she?"

"*Real* sick."

When we arrived there was a man worriedly waiting for us at the airport. He was a grown-up picture of a little boy with half-moon laughing eyes, who carried me piggyback and bought me ice cream. I didn't know whether to scream and run into his arms, jump up and down and cry, laugh and squeeze him, or kiss his cheeks with little-sister kisses so he would tell me everything would be okay, just as he did when I was little and Mommy was sick. I did none of those. I smiled and said, "Hello, Don."

Mother had cancer. She had felt bad for a long time but didn't have enough money to go to a doctor. She had no insurance, so she had avoided getting the necessary checkups and X rays. We learned she had gotten to the point where she couldn't work because she could barely breathe and she couldn't stand on her feet all day, so she went on welfare and social security. She was using food stamps and telling people she felt fine. One day, walking to the post office, she couldn't breathe and had to sit on the curb and ask someone to get her a taxi. She was only a block from where she lived. Finally, welfare paid for medical care and a tumor was discovered pushing on her trachea, bronchial tubes, and esophagus.

We rushed into the hospital in Evergreen Park, where a doctor met us. "I'm sorry to tell you this," he said, "but your mother is going to die. We'll do a biopsy, but I think surgery would be too much for her at this point. I'm afraid she would die on the table if we tried to remove the cancer now."

Steve panicked. "No! We've got to do something! I'll get a specialist! There's got to be something we can do." The three of us were crying silently, each alone in our own grief. We didn't touch or hug to comfort one another. We were almost strangers, grieving for a mother who was a different person to each of us. We sat waiting in her room later, the three of us, these two brothers I had loved and needed and waited for all my life, and I. If there was ever a time I wished I knew how to pray, it was then. Suddenly I burst, like a dam. I couldn't hold it any longer. I ran into the hallway, sobbing.

Steve arranged for a specialist to diagnose and treat Mother. Though she was too weak for surgery, she held on. She had always been a tiny person, but now she weighed about eighty pounds. She hadn't eaten for several weeks because of the tumor growing in her throat and neck. The injustice of her illness was more than we could stand. The doctor recommended radiation and her treatments began in the next few days. Miraculously, she started to improve.

David asked me later on the phone if I didn't think I should try to find my father and tell him about our wedding in July. He thought I should invite him.

I was stunned. "You've got to be kidding," I said. "My *father!*"

"Maybe you and he could have a relationship now."

"David, you can't be serious. I haven't seen him since I was eleven years old."

"Yes, but, he's still your father—"

"It amazes me how you people who have normal families just can't understand how a person feels about a parent who dumped them."

"Maybe you're being too hard on him, Cathy."

"I don't believe you're saying this to me."

"I'm sure he thought he was doing the right thing for you. I just don't think he knew how much you were suffering."

"He never listened to me when I told him how I felt. On my eleventh birthday he showed up and gave me a pearl ring. He never told me he wasn't going to see me again. I haven't seen him in nine years. He took me to lunch, gave me a ring, and left me. Boy, when I have kids, I'll love them so much. I'll never leave them."

"I think we should invite your father to the wedding. Do you think he'll come?"

"I don't know."

"Let's invite him."

"What if he refuses? Do you know what that would do to me? It would break my heart. At least with him out of my life it isn't constant rejection. At least I never get my hopes up. Can't you understand?"

"I still think we should invite him to the wedding. I can't imagine that he wouldn't want to come and see his daughter married."

I was amazed at what I heard. He was so purehearted. Maybe he was right. I hoped he was right!

"Do you think—"

"It just might be the beginning of a relationship for you two. Somebody has to make a first move. Why shouldn't it be you?"

I wasn't going to try to find my father, but Steve did. He called the Missing Persons Department and tracked him down. He was given the telephone number and dialed it. A woman's voice answered. Steve asked for my father.

"Who's calling?"

"Steve Crowell."

The telephone was dropped suddenly and Steve could hear screaming in the background.

A man's voice was then heard on the other end of the line. He was calm and businesslike and a meeting was arranged for lunch.

We met at a place called Petros Restaurant on Randolph and Deerborn across the street from the Bismarck Hotel. Steve, Don, and I crossed the traffic-crammed street to the restaurant, where the menu was taped on the window. Don led me inside. The booths were mustard-colored plastic and we slid into one. Then I saw him. His face was soft, lined, not like I expected it to be, and he was bald. He was cordial but nervous. I asked him at one point in a vague and cluttered exchange of dull, clumsy words, "Did you ever think about what you were missing when you left me with Nellie Landers?"

His answer was, "No."

Later in the conversation he congratulated me on my upcoming marriage and suggested we not have children. "You can be happy without children," he said cheerfully.

I remembered David's encouraging words, so I hesitantly invited him to the wedding.

He answered swiftly. "No."

"But don't you want to see your daughter get married?" Don asked.

"Well, there will be people there I don't want to see."

I got courageous—desperate, really. "You could sneak in the back and sit where nobody can see you!"

He refused.

He was looking at his watch. "I'm twenty years old," I offered in a high, cracked voice. "It's been nine years since I've seen you. Do you realize what you did to me?"

His face registered a shimmer of surprise. "Why, no," he replied.

I continued. "Isn't it a little strange that your children can't call you at your home?" (Pat had made my father tell Steve never to call there again.) When I said that, my father got the same look on his face he has in the photograph I have of him when he was in the navy.

"My wife loves me intensely," was his comment.

He took out his wallet, and I saw he had five or six pictures of me as a little girl. There was a picture of me in pigtails outside Nellie's place in Michigan, another one taken at a studio. They were buried under cards and other photos. "Cathy, I want you to know that I intend to do something for you. I know you've had it the hardest of you kids."

"It's too late," I said.

He gave me a look like when I was a little girl and we were walking down the street together, and he said, "Turn your feet in." Forever after I never walked with turned-out feet.

Then, from out of nowhere, his eyes blurred red. He started crying and whispered, "Cathy, you look so much like my mother—you're just the image of her. She wore her hair just like you do, up in a French braid. . . ."

I felt nothing. After that I remembered hardly anything of the conversation.

My mother's health improved enough in the next couple of weeks for her to come back to New Hampshire with us. I refused to let her stay alone. She protested because she didn't want to leave her friends, but I convinced her to come so we could take care of her. In March of 1981, my mother flew to New Hampshire.

We found her an apartment on Main Street in Antrim near us in one of the big old three-story houses that lined the street. Hers was on the third floor. It had a bedroom, a living room, a kitchenette, a bathroom, and a walk-in closet with no door. There were only two windows, so even on breezy days it was hot and stuffy with no cross ventilation. But it was the best place we could find for forty-five dollars a week.

It was an adjustment having my mother near me. I was afraid she wouldn't get well, but I wouldn't admit it. I continued to work at Brookstone, and she watched by her window as I left in the morning and when I drove by on my way home every night. By the time I got in the door, my phone was eagerly ringing.

We had her over for dinner, or I would take her out for lunch, or we went shopping together; sometimes she just came over and sat and watched while I cleaned the apartment.

In July we drove back to Chicago to prepare for the wedding. Invitations had been sent out weeks before. I had even contacted Mark Smith to ask him if he thought Carol and Bernie would feel offended if I sent them an invitation also. He suggested I make an attempt, which I did. I expected my wedding day to be the happiest day of my life. It was. My mother was there, dressed in a beautiful blue pleated gown with a white flowing lace cape bodice. Uncle Bill gave me away. It was a large wedding at Saint Joseph's Church, where I had attended (when I attended) during my years in Homewood. The reception was held at David's parents' home and it was magnificent, complete with a white latticed gazebo to house a giant tiered wedding cake. I wore a lace gown and a long lace veil and had my hair twisted in a French braid on the back of my head. David was as handsome as Cinderella's prince, and that was how I felt—like Cinderella. There were three dark spots on our special day: Carol and Bernie and my father refused to come to the wedding. But I wouldn't allow the dark spots to overshadow my joy. David's warm and loving family surrounded me and filled every minute of the day. I gave myself into their care.

Before we returned to New Hampshire as Mr. and Mrs. David Webb, we were able to reestablish a relationship with Carol and Bernie and the boys. This relationship was on a more mature level. From then on we exchanged correspondence and phone calls. Carol and

Bernie even visited us once, and were always generous to us and our children.

I enrolled at the University of New Hampshire in Durham to begin classes in the fall of 1981. My mother thought it was a great idea because that meant we might all move there, and David fully approved because he was eager to get on with his education, too. My mother was still smoking heavily and the air in her small apartment, with its poor ventilation, was always thick with brown clouds of smoke. I worried about the cancer. It seemed she was smoking more than ever. She didn't have many activities or interests. She was too frail for physical acitivites and she didn't like to sew; reading was just not appealing to her because she didn't like to sit still that long, and her TV didn't get good reception. The thing she wanted most in her life was to be near me.

19

Antrim

I DIDN'T KNOW what to expect of a Baptist Bible study. I
wondered if it would be like a confirmation class or a
CCD class. On a Wednesday night toward the end of
August, I drove to the small historic town of Peterborough to the Odd Fellows' Hall, a white clap-
board building. I pulled into a dirt parking lot and
climbed the steps. Inside I paused to look around. In the
room where the Bible study was held there was a platform up front with a white podium, backed by a couple
of faded ornate chairs. Below the podium folding chairs
were arranged in rows. I sat down in one of them on the
far right.

The meeting started when the pastor mounted the
platform. He was a man of medium height, an
American-born Italian with green eyes, a prominent
nose, and full head of dark, curly hair. A piano I hadn't
noticed suddenly came alive as a melody was tapped out
by a lady in a cotton print dress. Everyone rose and
began to sing. I did, too, although I didn't know the
words.

I serve a risen Savior, He's in the world today;
I know that He is living, whatever man may say;
I see His hand of mercy. I hear His voice of cheer,
and just the time I need Him He's always near.

I listened to the voices of the dozen or so people, scattered, squeaking on the high parts, and, keeping my eyes on the songbook, sang along: "He lives, He lives, Christ Jesus lives today. . . ."

The walls of the room were painted dull green and lined with pictures of Odd Fellows. We sat after the song and the pastor began to teach the Bible study. I tried to listen and understand, but I felt out of place. He was teaching people who obviously had some Bible background. I felt like a child who had walked into a college class.

A familiar fear struck me. I remembered it as if I were back in fourth grade when Aunt Nellie dropped me off in front of the church to attend mass before I went to school. I remembered it so clearly, me smiling at Aunt Nellie and saying good-bye and going in to listen to a mass I knew by heart, backward and forward. I worried about never being good enough to please God. I worried I'd never get to go to heaven. As a child I sat in church, twisting my fingers together, agonizing over walking out of the holy church doors and never being good enough to please God.

I twisted my fingers now.

The following Monday night I rushed home after work and baked my best recipe for chocolate chip cookies. David came home from work at about six o'clock because he had a job fairly close by. We had a quick dinner and then at seven o'clock there was a knock at the door. It was Pastor Carl Nannini and his wife, Bonnie. "It's so nice of you to invite us to stop by, Cathy," Mrs. Nannini smiled. "Last Wednesday as you were leaving, I just knew you had some more questions."

Bonnie Nannini had an animated smile and penetrating blue eyes. She wore light lipstick and a trace of eye shadow, and her light brown hair feathered softly over her ears. "What a darling place you have!" she exclaimed once we were seated in the living room. We chatted for a while and when I learned they had six children I inwardly groaned. I didn't want to have children for a long time. I wanted a career. I was going to make something of myself; I told them I had enrolled at the University of New Hampshire in Durham. Our plan was that I would start school first and David would resume his studies later. The Nanninis sat on the sofa and David sat in the wicker chair in the corner. I served the cookies and coffee and sat cross-legged on the floor. "Tell me about the Bible," I said.

"The Bible is the inspired Word of God," Pastor Nannini began. "Some people think it's just a storybook or a book teaching us how to be good people. Actually, the Bible is far more. The Bible comes from a divine Source, from God Himself."

"I thought Moses wrote it."

The pastor then explained how Moses was one of the instruments God used to speak through in the Bible. Moses is the author of the first five books of the Old Testament, called the Pentateuch. John 1:1 says, "In the beginning was the Word, and the Word was with God, and the Word was God."

I looked over at David. After working a full day in the hot sun, he did what I was afraid he'd do: he fell asleep and missed the whole conversation.

Mrs. Nannini spoke next. "Think how God made it so easy for us to know Him in First John 5:13:

These things have I written unto you that believe on
the name of the Son of God; that ye may know that
ye have eternal life, and that ye may believe on the
name of the Son of God.

His Word, the Bible, is written to show us the way to Him and heaven."

I learned something I had never heard before: I learned that from the very first page of the Bible to the last page, its theme is redemption, because "All have sinned, and come short of the glory of God" (Romans

3:23). God wants to redeem people to Himself.

There is a penalty to pay: "For the wages of sin is death; but the gift of God is eternal life through Jesus Christ our Lord" (Romans 6:23). There is a picture of the Messiah Jesus Christ, anticipated in the Old Testament and realized in the New Testament. It is a crimson thread running from the Book of Genesis through the Book of Revelation, and it leads to the cross of Jesus Christ. "Without the shedding of blood there is no remission of sins."

I was silent. What I was hearing seemed so far away. Were mere words going to make me a better person or get me closer to God? I grew up believing that Jesus was part of the Holy Trinity, and that He died on the cross to open the gates of heaven. Then it was my job to get there by being good. So, how would the Bible get me closer to God?

I asked that question and Pastor Nannini answered. "A person can read the Bible and not have a personal relationship with God. There is no way to be accepted by God without Jesus Christ. In John 14:6 Jesus said, 'I am the way, the truth, and the life: no man cometh unto the Father, but by me.' In other words, the way to God is not through our own perfection, but through Jesus Christ. God loved us enough to send His only Son, that we who believe in Him as our Savior will have everlasting life."

I explained how I had gone to church and had always wanted to be good so I could get to heaven. But I knew I had done bad things. I didn't tell them how Liz and I used to steal Aunt Nellie's offering envelopes and skip church to go eat junk food down the street . . . nor did I tell them about the man in jail. I told them of my thirst for knowledge about God. I never seemed to be able to find Him. I never felt I was good enough for His acceptance.

"You need salvation from sin. Let me tell you what that means. Cathy, have you ever sinned?"

"Of course," I answered, imagining that God had a large scale. The good things were weighed on one side, the bad things on the other. There had always been a problem: The bad things weighed more.

Then the pastor talked about when Jesus was born in a manger in Bethlehem. He began to fulfill the prophecies of the Old Testament regarding the coming Messiah. Jesus would become the substitute for our sins. Jesus Himself was sinless. Born of the Holy Spirit in the Virgin Mary's body, He is God and became man to be our substitute for our sin.

"Only someone absolutely sinless could take on Himself every sin of the world. The Bible explains salvation when it tells us in Romans 5:8, 'But God commendeth his love toward us, in that, while we were yet sinners, Christ died for us.' Jesus is the only way to have your sins forgiven. He can give you perfect peace. It's called being born again."

"Born again?"

"Let me tell you about another Bible passage. It's found in the Book of John in the New Testament. One night a rich young ruler sneaked out of his house and found Jesus in order to talk with Him. He knew that Jesus was from God because he saw the miracles He performed. Jesus told him, 'Except a man be born again, he cannot see the kingdom of God.' Jesus wanted Nicodemus to understand, 'That which is born of the flesh is flesh and that which is born of the spirit is spirit.' There's a God-sized hole in every one of us, and it can only be filled by Christ."

"How does that happen?"

"By asking the Lord Jesus into your heart. Do you want to be forgiven for your sins?"

"Oh, I used to ask that all the time," I said. "I would try to figure out how I could please God. I knew there must be a way, so I tried everything I could to be perfect. But then, I guess it was around the sixth grade, after failing so many times, I gave up."

"God gave us His greatest gift of all when He gave us Jesus Christ. Jesus came to give us a new birth, so we can be born in the Spirit. Being born again is the experience of receiving new life through Jesus Christ."

We talked until about eleven o'clock. Pastor Nannini turned to one more Scripture verse in his Bible. He handed it to me and said, "Cathy, would you read this verse out loud, please?" It was Ephesians 2:8 and 9. I took his Bible and read: "For by grace are ye saved through faith: and that not of yourselves: it is the gift of God: not of works, lest any man should boast. . . ." It was as though a light clicked on. A *gift*. I thought I had to work for God's approval. I thought I had to prove myself first before He would even consider me as anything worthwhile.

"Do you know what grace is? Grace is God's undeserved favor, His unmerited love. Galatians 2:21 says, 'I do not frustrate the grace of God: for if righteousness come by the law, then Christ is dead in vain.' God's love for us is entirely undeserved on our part, but it is a free gift from God. His grace is what allows us to come to Him, not our good deeds."

I sat there on the floor, staring at the words in the Bible, amazed. Why hadn't I heard about this before?

The pastor asked me gently, "Do you want to ask the Lord Jesus into your heart, Cathy?" I nodded. Yes, I did. Without even waiting for them to begin a prayer, I bowed my head and prayed, "Lord Jesus, I know that I am a bad sinner and I want you to be my Savior. I really need a Savior. I believe You died on the cross to pay for all my sins. Forgive me, Lord. My sins put You on that cross." When I lifted my head my face was red with embarrassment because I realized someone was watching me as I prayed.

David awoke as they left and when they were gone I told him, "Guess what, David? I accepted Christ as my Savior." He looked at me blankly but then he helped me bring the coffee cups into the kitchen and he leaned against the counter and smiled at me. "Well, how do you feel?"

"At peace."

The next morning I couldn't wait to get up and read the little Bible the Nanninis had left with us. I read, "For by grace are ye saved through faith; and that not of yourself: it is a gift of God . . ." again and again. Driving to work I felt as if I were floating, flying. I prayed out loud, "Thank You for forgiving me!"

Neither is there salvation in any other: for there is none other name under heaven given among men, whereby we must be saved (Acts 4:12).

I began naming sins I had committed. "Forgive me," I prayed. "That sin put You on the cross. Thank You for forgiving me." The discovery of God was wonderful; it was glorious! Another sin came to mind. "Forgive me! That sin put You on the cross, too." Another and another—I knew I was now close to God and accepted by Him, just as the pastor had explained. I was practically ecstatic. Then as suddenly as a blast from a rifle, and as ferocious, I saw a man. His shoulders were shaking; he was sobbing before a judge. *Oh, God, no, not that, please! Not that!*

The joy left me.

A curtain fell and as I drove over the crest of the hill by the side of the mountains to the turnoff, I knew that God had full knowledge of the one sin I couldn't face, and I also knew I could never be close to God again until I made it right, but my old pattern intervened and I put it out of my mind. I shut my Bible every time I came upon a sin I didn't want to face.

I also discovered I was pregnant.

David attended the little church in Peterborough with me. After each service Pastor Nannini made a point to talk personally with him. He told David, "When you give your heart to the Lord Jesus Christ and become a Christian, I can call you my brother." Then the next week, when he saw David, he asked, "May I call you brother yet?" David always answered, "No, not yet."

When we were dating we liked to talk about religion, especially Eastern religion. David took his time considering Jesus Christ as the only way to God. When we talked about it, we realized neither of us had discovered that Zen or "religion" did anything for us from the inside out. There was no life to Zen, just philosophy. Religion in general isn't what connects us to God—it's God Himself. When David saw that Jesus Christ was the expression of God on earth as His only begotten Son, and as the living Word and Savior—then he was able to see his need for the Lord. Becoming a Christian is not just embracing some principles, it's saying yes to the Lord Jesus Christ as Savior and Lord of your life, and then living by the power of His Spirit. In October of that year David and I talked a lot about God and His plan for redemption.

"I don't think I could ever earn my way to heaven," David said one day.

"Me neither, David. That's why I accepted Christ as my Savior."

"You mean you got *saved?*"

"Yes."

"That's what I want, too."

I'll never know why God has chosen to bless me the way He has. I'll never understand His mercy and His kindness. He didn't throw me away on the garbage bin of life for what I did to Gary Dotson. He helped me become a new person and a healthy, sound-thinking, free one. When David became a Christian, we started a new journey together, one that we promised would belong to God.

The next Sunday morning in church we sang:

Great is thy faithfulness,
God my Father,
There is no shadow of turning with thee;
Thou changest not, thy compassions they fail not;
As thou hast been thou forever wilt be.

I didn't know the power and depth of that song. I didn't know how really great His faithfulness to me was—but I was beginning to find out.

Great is thy faithfulness!
Great is thy faithfulness!
Morning by morning new mercies I see;
All I have needed thy hand hath provided—
Great is thy faithfulness,
Lord, unto me!

1982

In May of 1982 David and I became the parents of a little pink-faced boy named Andrew. My mother was thrilled. She sat holding him by the hour, just rocking and holding him. She was still affectionate and it still embarrassed me. I would never go up to her and give her a hug just for the heck of it; I wouldn't tell her I loved her, even though I knew that was what she wanted and needed. Something stopped me. I just couldn't.

Sometimes when we talked I wanted to bring up the past, but we rarely mentioned it. On the few occasions when we did, she never expressed anger or bitterness toward anyone or anything. I guess she thought I felt the same way she did.

Maybe I didn't show it, but I *was* angry and I *was* bitter. Mother's one simple statement summing up all those lost years was, "That Nellie was a witch." I had much more to say than that, but I didn't. My mother was a gentle person and I didn't want to upset her. But the thoughts and feelings a person has inside come out, even if you don't want them to. I was distant from her; it was as if we stood on opposite sides of a wall of glass. I couldn't reach out to her, couldn't take hold of her silvery presence. It confused me and made me feel guilty. Here I was, at last, with my mother, the one I had dreamed of every night as a little girl, but I couldn't touch her. I told myself it was because I was older now. I could bake my own cookies, tie my own shoes, and hug my own baby at night.

She wore Emeraude perfume and when I took her shopping to Peterborough or another nearby town, she put on double-knit pants and a ribbed-knit shirt and looked young, almost healthy. She always wore bright-red lipstick. She loved going places with me. Her tragic eyes would search my face at times, as though trying to understand what was going on inside my head. Usually I kept the conversation light, on trivial things, so she wouldn't ask questions. Her thin, imploring hands held my arm as we walked.

By now I was pregnant again and David was out of town working most of the time. In fact, he missed out on most of Andrew's first year because his work took him to building sites too far away to commute back and forth. He came home only on weekends.

Mother and I went to church together and she enjoyed it. She liked the people and they liked her. But I had pulled away from her. I was there in body only. I was known as a moody person so she probably just figured I was being moody. But it was more than moodiness, it was fear—fear of losing what was most precious to me. Now that we finally had each other, I was terrified she was going to leave me.

She began chemotherapy treatment with a cancer specialist in Manchester. The tumor was growing back.

"The doctor in Manchester is a kind man. He's one of the best specialists in the country, you know," Mother told me one day as she gazed out her window.

He knew my mother didn't have any money, but he still treated her well. She thrived on care and attention. She loved to be picked up to go places on the spur of the moment. I'd call and say, "Mom, I'm going to Keene, want to go with me?" And she'd be ready in no time. It was a real thrill for her.

David and I started looking for a house in January of 1983. I was so pregnant, and David was home so little, but I knew it was important to find a house. My mother had not mentioned her "special dream" from years ago. But I was searching for a wooden house with trees around it; one that had a room that would be her very own. . . .

It was the strangest thing, though. Sometimes when

Mother knocked on the door I didn't want to answer it. And when I did, I hardly talked to her and my attitude was hard and cold. She would just love to come up and give me a big hug right out of nowhere, or kiss me and say, "I love you." And I would just freeze. I felt *scared*. (David couldn't understand it. He thought I was just horrible.)

Finally we found a house in Jaffrey—a house with wood siding and oak wood floors and a room especially for Mom. I went to work decorating it exactly as she would like it. I told myself, *She's not going to die. When we move into our own house and she has her own room, she won't die. I'll fix her room exactly the way she wants it.*

I watched her grow worse and I prayed continually. One day she went shopping with Bonnie Nannini and something exciting happened. I could tell by her face when she came in the door.

"Cathy! I understand what you've been telling me about Jesus. I didn't quite get it before—how God gives us salvation as a free gift. I thought I wasn't good enough to have what you and your friends have. I thought I already had as much faith as I needed because I prayed and went to church. *Now*, I really understand. Your pastor's wife explained all that you've been telling me."

I felt tears come to my eyes. To hear her say those words and to know how many years she had suffered—now she would have the peace she had always looked for and always wanted.

"I'm not a bad person," she continued, "because the Bible says that His grace is sufficient for me and His strength is made perfect in weakness. I gave my life to Jesus Christ, and Cathy, I'm so happy."

Fear left me. I knew now no matter what happened, I would see my mother again. I could face her impending death without the agony of losing her for all eternity. But still . . .

1983

I was quite big at the end of the pregnancy and came close to toxemia. I was retaining water and my blood pressure was high. Pastor and Bonnie had my mother stay at their house and she was treated like a queen. We were getting ready for us all to move into the house we had just bought. Mom loved the house and she was so happy about it.

There were at least seventeen people from the church helping us move that weekend. They wanted me to be able to spend time with my mom because they all knew how sick she was. She was at the end, and still I couldn't face it. Bonnie called me up and said, "Why don't you come over and see your mom now?" I said I would be right there, but it took me two hours to get there. I felt as if I was being swallowed by something horrible and huge. There was no way to hold on to her—to make her well—to *keep* her.

One week later at the Nannini home, Mother sat propped up in bed with pillows, praying and counting her blessings. "What woman could ask for more than I have, Lord Jesus? I'm a Nana and a Mom. My children love me and that's the best gift of all."

Pastor Nannini told me later that on Saturday morning, May 20, 1983, my mother came downstairs to talk to him.

"I hope I don't scare you without my wig on," she laughed. The pastor laughed, too, and prepared them both some coffee. They sat down on the sofa together and Mother talked a little bit about her life, how since the divorce she had lived most of her life in rented rooms, boarding houses, or in hospitals.

She had dreamed all those years of getting her children back, of being married again to someone who loved her and her family. She had especially dreamed of her little girl. All those years! But now God had given her daughter back to her. She had everything she wanted. She knew she was ready to see God. She had found peace and happiness.

"Pastor, I think I'm ready to go meet Jesus. I'm prepared now and I'm looking forward to it." The compassionate man sitting beside her put his arms around her and held her. There wasn't a tremor in her body, not a quiver of fear. They prayed together then and Mom smiled a warm, contented smile. She was ready.

20

Jaffrey
1983

MY MOTHER DIED May 21, 1983, two days before her fifty-third birthday, and two weeks before I gave birth to our second baby, Elizabeth. Her favorite dress had been the long blue pleated one with the white lace bodice cape that she wore to our wedding. I knew she'd want to be buried in it, so I went to her apartment to get it from the closet. Her smells still lingered in the rooms: musty, stale smoke and the tiniest hint of Emeraude. I went to her doorless closet and, looking at the few things hanging there, I pulled out the dress I had come for. It was full of nicotine! It was yellow stained! All the smoke of the apartment must have collected in that closet because everything was stained yellow. Everything! The lovely white lace bodice cape looked aged and it smelled like smoke. I scrubbed and scrubbed the lace. I used special powders and liquids to remove stains, but it never did become clean enough to use. I was frantic. Finally I found another dress that didn't show the yellow as badly, and even though I couldn't get the smell out entirely, it was acceptable. So my mother was buried in an acceptable dress and people commented on how nice she looked. The picture I will always carry in my heart is

of her wearing her long blue pleated dress with the
bright white lace cape top. Her twinkling eyes are smiling directly at me.

We bought the old house in Jaffrey on Farmer's
Loan. It had been built as a summer cottage in 1928. It
needed a lot of work, but we told ourselves we had all
the time in the world to do it. One of the best things
about the house was its closeness to our church, which
had been completed the previous September. The congregation had worked hard, saved, and bought the land
to build a church, and now our prayers were answered
and we had our very own building to meet in.

So there were lots of new things—new baby, new
home, new church, new beginnings. The people at
church had shown my mother love and tender care in
her last two years. My brothers were surprised at all the
people who showed up at her funeral. They didn't
realize she had so many friends. "She was a dear lady,
and we all loved her," a church friend told them.

At night I cried, feeling helpless, as though I were a
baby again when she went away. She had been with me
for so little time! And now it was over, just before our
dream came true, our wooden house with white ruffled
curtains.

1984

The winter of 1984 folded in around us like a cloak. I
stayed inside our New England cottage with two babies
and a wood-burning stove while David worked his usual
long, hard days, rising at three-thirty in the morning to
go to work and returning at seven-thirty at night, six
days a week. My Bible lay untouched by the bed. There
was a slow, rising tension in me, one I was hardly aware
of until I found myself losing my temper at slight distur-
bances.

I knew I could ignore unpleasant thoughts if I just
held on. I tried to make sense of my daily chores and the
importance of the life around me. I polished my copper

skillet and molded bowl and hung them on the brick of the fireplace. I had started to collect brass and copper. I thought it would be fun to fill the brick with antique copper skillets and bowls. I busied myself, making our home as attractive and clean as I could. I told myself it was important to keep busy.

I wouldn't allow the Lord to comfort me with His Word. "Fear thou not: for I am with thee: be not dismayed, for I am thy God and I will strengthen thee; yea, I will help thee; yea, I will uphold thee with the right hand of my righteousness." I needed strength; I had only to reach out to take Him. The two children exhausted me, I grieved for my mother, and God was working on my conscience. This was the worst part. He was forcing something up and out of a deep, hidden place in me, something buried that I couldn't face. At times I would feel like running, but looking at the trusting faces of my little children, I knew I couldn't leave. I found comfort in the love of my friends from church. We shared baby-sitting, housekeeping hints, recipes, and our feelings about the lives we led. I was glad they were there because of the long hours David worked, and at least I had someone to talk to, even if it was mostly about diaper rash and teething rings. Someone was always available to pray whenever there was a need. That was sort of an unnerving aspect of the closeness of the women. At times it was comfortable to ask them to pray for me, but at other times I tried to hide my feelings unless it was absolutely impossible, and even then, I would not reveal the real thing that was bothering me.

The *real* thing? The real thing tormented me months later. It was spring 1984. David and the children and I were on a picnic in the mountains by a little stream. Along the banks of the forest stream were purple trillium. Black-eyed Susans, daisies, and budding mountain laurel dotted the meadow where we spread out our blanket. I had packed sandwiches on homemade wheat bread, soda crackers, orange juice, and a thermos of coffee. As a special treat, I had baked oatmeal raisin cookies that morning and I brought them along to surprise David. Instead of enjoying the beautiful day and the time with my husband and children, I nagged at him and complained, wasting the few precious moments we had together during the week as a family.

"I know it's hard," David was saying. "But I don't know what else to do. I have to make a living, don't I?" I tried to make him the reason for all my unrest. It was because of his long hours, our lack of money, I complained. That's why I was so moody.

"I'm working as hard as I can, Cathy, and that's why I like to take overtime when I can get it—so we can get ahead."

David didn't like to hear about troubles. He was a person who had few bad feelings and little animosity toward any living soul. He was so easygoing and genuinely trusting that it made him uneasy to hear about my inner struggles. He usually changed the subject if I started telling him about my troubles. He just wanted everyone to be happy. He had a brilliant mind and had been a top student before he quit college, but he just didn't like to talk about personal, emotional troubles.

He was upset now. Our picnic was ruined. He could see I was in a bad mood and he was taking the blame for it. "I'm an ironworker's widow," I complained. "I'm home six days a week with the kids and no husband and no help."

"Cathy, I think we really need to pray about this— together. The Lord will help us and show us what to do."

He prayed but I didn't want to, even though I felt guilty about nagging him. I couldn't shake the feeling that our problems were somehow due to something I was doing wrong. There was something that the Lord was not pleased with and instead of blaming David for it, I should have praised and loved my husband. He wasn't to blame. When I was alone I started praying and asking the Lord to help me be the kind of wife I should be. I wanted to be the kind of wife that pleased God. I read Proverbs 31, "She opened her mouth with wisdom; and in her tongue is the law of kindness." I thought to myself, *I am a nag and a nitpicker and sarcastic to my husband.* I felt convicted and asked God to forgive me. "Lord Jesus, please help me to be the kind of woman who has kindness and wisdom in her mouth."

I began to see motherhood as an honorable and noble profession that God had called me to. I didn't just love my children, now I enjoyed them.

"Boy, have I changed," I chuckled to myself. It used to be that I wanted to take the world by storm; be a successful executive. Now here I was living in an old wood frame house out in the sticks of New Hampshire, hauling in wood for a stove, baking bread, and buying milk from the farmer next door. I was even starting to enjoy homemaking. We didn't have a TV set and didn't want one. Who would have guessed I could change so much? Just at that moment, the black-and-white spotted cow in the field next door nudged her way up to the side and mooed long and plaintively. I turned, but I thought I saw another scene—not a field, but a wooded park, a piece of broken glass, a torn sailor blouse, a navy knee-high crumpled around a toe. *My God! What am I doing to myself?*

21

As Easter 1984 approached, David and I planned for our future and the future of our children at the small, square table in the middle of the oak-floored dining area. We told our friends, "We bought this house so we could have our grandchildren and great-grandchildren in it. We didn't buy it to fix it up and sell it for profit in order to move somewhere else. This is where we want to stay, unless God directs us otherwise." We talked and we planned. Outwardly everything was calm, but inside I was growing more restless. Keeping constantly busy seemed to make it easier for me to avoid an ominous warning in my mind. Every day I awoke early to sit alone at that same small table and read my Bible. It was as if I was compelled to find something, learn something, gain something meant especially for me. Alone with God each morning, I began to question what it meant to be a Christian. I knew it wasn't simply a change of life-style—throwing out my blue jeans in favor of dresses and skirts; it wasn't only not swearing or telling off-color jokes; it wasn't giving up drinking and an immoral life. No, these things had been taken care of soon after my salvation. These changes of outward appearance, behavior, and life-style were because God had given me new desires. They were the fruit of my faith in God. But something was missing. . . .

On Easter morning we had pancakes and orange juice; I gave Andrew and Elizabeth their vitamins, then I cleared the dishes while David hustled the kids upstairs to dress in the cleaned and pressed clothes I had laid out for them. As I worked, I kept thinking about the Scripture verses I had studied earlier that morning, Matthew 11:28–30:

> *Come unto me, all ye that labour and are heavy laden, and I will give you rest. Take my yoke upon you, and learn of me; for I am meek and lowly in heart; and ye shall find rest unto your souls. For my yoke is easy, and my burden is light.*

I let the words sink in. "Yes," I sighed softly, "I understand, Lord." He had saved me from the penalty of sin, and He gave me a place in His kingdom. But there was something more that I had not thought about. In order to be yoked with Him, I would have to walk right next to Him, so that He could direct my life. I knew I had never really done that because I didn't want to let go of my selfish, prideful controls. Right there in my kitchen, on Easter morning, I asked Jesus to be not only my Savior but the Lord of my life as well. My prayer was a single sentence: "Yes, I want You to be my Lord, now."

Things changed for me after that Easter Sunday. When I awoke in the morning, instead of complaining to myself about David, I prayed and asked the Lord what I could do for him that day that would be special. I promised Jesus I wouldn't nag him to change jobs because of his long hours and time away from home, even though I was really worried about him. Twice he had fallen asleep behind the wheel of the car, and I was afraid that he might be injured on some construction project. But I knew he was struggling to do his best for our family. I told the Lord, "Your yoke is easy and Your burden is light. You be the Lord of this problem. If it's Your will, find David another job."

The next weeks were wonderful. I prayed and read
from the Bible from half-past five in the morning until
the children woke up for breakfast. And then after I
washed the dishes, I'd be right back studying the Word
again. I felt close to the Lord.

David was still working night and day, and we were
still over our heads in debt, but I had a certain peace
about our situation. I made a special project of collect-
ing low-budget recipes and learning how to cook with
soybeans and tofu, brown rice and ground meal. Fresh
fruit was something we could only occasionally afford.
By using coupons and buying only where the prices were
cheapest, we could keep our food budget at one hundred dollars a month or less. Some months we had only
seventy dollars to spend on food. I cooked a healthy
breakfast cereal of four grains I bought at a food co-op.
We called it "Mighty Mush." The children and I took
advantage of the clothes which the mothers at church
passed around. At Christmastime, David's parents and
my brother Steve and his family gave us a new freezer
full of beef and pork. I marveled at the way God provided for our needs, but I refused to acknowledge that
the reason God did not bless us was that I was withholding total obedience.

I hung my clothes out on the line and looked over the
back pasture to the forest of spruce, oak, and white pine
growing tall along the river below. Wood and meadow
lilies bloomed at the edge of the fence and down the
pasture, where the cows grazed peacefully, moving their
bodies slowly, languidly, as they chewed. I was totally
immersed in the routine of life. I washed the white ruffled curtains, clipped coupons, organized the children's
clothes, baked cookies using honey instead of sugar. I
thought of my mother and how she had rarely complained. I remembered the hours I spent with her at the
hospital, reading the Bible to her. She never once complained about pain or discomfort. She didn't complain
about that awful little apartment in Antrim. She didn't
complain about her hair falling out. She was the sweet-

est person I had ever known . . . I wished I had known
her longer.

When I thought about her, the Word began to fill my
heart. I had to learn how to be close to God and be obedient to Him as well. I read John 15:4 and 5:

> *Abide in me, and I in you. As the branch cannot
> bear fruit of itself, except it abide in the vine; no
> more can ye, except ye abide in me. I am the vine,
> ye are the branches: He that abideth in me, and I in
> him, the same bringeth forth much fruit: for
> without me ye can do nothing.*

Time was passing, and I was learning. Later that summer, our congregation held a rummage sale to help raise
funds for our new church building. I polished up the
brass and copper collection that I loved so much and
donated it for the cause. At first I believed that God
would not let it sell. I figured He was just testing me to
see if I would be willing to get rid of it for His sake. This
was all a part of learning that He was in charge of my
life. I wondered if God was telling me that my collection
was too important to me.

The day of the sale, I left my precious collection on
the grass with little price tags taped on each piece.
Swallowing dryness, with one last look at the beautiful
copper piece David's mother had given me, I said softly,
"These are all Yours, Jesus. I'm making You the Lord
of my life and everything I own, too." I meant it.

About a month later, though, I received a gift for my
birthday from my "Secret Pal" at church. It was a large
shopping bag stuffed with heavy items. A note taped on
the inside of the bag read: "With love to my Secret Pal.
Happy Birthday." I opened the bag and there was my
copper and brass collection. God had used my Secret
Pal to start building a faith and trust in Him that I
needed.

There was still more to learn. When Bonnie asked me to

help with her Sunday-school class, I refused for selfish reasons. After a long internal struggle with God, I finally agreed to participate, though I was not totally willing. Each week I sat in a daze as the children listened to Bible stories and learned verses. One day I was suddenly brought out of my stupor when I heard Galatians 6:7 read:

> *Be not deceived; God is not mocked: for whatsoever a man soweth, that shall he also reap.*

It was a stab in the heart. Did that mean that my family would suffer as *his* family had suffered? To make matters worse, the children sang a song called "Obedience Is." One of the choruses went: "Obedience is the best way to show that you believe," and then all those fresh-faced children sang out loud and clear: "O-B-E-D-I-E-N-C-E." I hated that song.

Then Bonnie told a story about obedience: the story of Cain and Abel. Abel killed a sheep for God, because He wanted an animal sacrifice, but Cain merely gave the best fruits of his fields, when God had specifically told him He wanted a blood sacrifice. God was not happy because Cain did not give what He wanted. I also was not giving God what He wanted.

Through this little story for children, God was impressing me with the need to make things right. My natural response was, "No, I can't," but then I prayed, "Make me willing; give me the right desire."

Because I began to pray in His will, God showed me again that He wasn't going to give up on me, and that He loved me. I was like a child drinking in the love of a lost parent.

It wasn't long after that when David and I were driving home from church and he turned to me and said, "How would you like it if I changed jobs?" I caught my breath. He continued. "You haven't said anything lately, but I've been thinking, maybe if I worked for a different company I wouldn't have to work such long hours and go to such faraway building sites. Is that all right with you?'' Was that all right? I was overjoyed. God had answered my prayer.

1985

Christmas had come and gone, but even the celebration of the birth of Christ couldn't give me the joy that was missing in my heart. The colored lights, the smell of pine, the gifts and decorations I had made with my girlfriend from church were not sweet memories; they were just time fillers and I knew it.

I knew that God loved me, but something was still missing. David's parents had visited after the holidays, and I'm sure they went home concerned about my moodiness. You see, God was helping me build the desire to do right, and as that desire built, I was feeling guilt because of my lack of action.

I plunged back into business. There weren't enough hours in the day to do all the work I laid out for myself to accomplish. I washed windows, kept the house even cleaner, was nicer to David, cooked better and more economical meals, organized my cupboards into military order. I answered every request made of me at church. But these substitute acts of obedience were not appeasing or pleasing to God. And He constantly reminded me of that . . . especially with these words from 1 Samuel 15:22: ''. . . to obey is better than sacrifice. . . .''

Nights were bad for me. One night, when the fire had burned low, I awoke from a troubled sleep. I reached for David's arm; it was cold so I pulled the blanket up over his shoulder. He was cold; the room was cold, but I was flushed with heat. My forehead was sweaty; I felt damp all over. I wasn't sick but something was bothering me. I slipped out of bed and tiptoed into Elizabeth's room and peeked over the edge of the crib at her. She

was curled in the corner holding her "blankee" with the
frayed edges to her face.

I stroked her cheek and smoothed her hair. So precious! What if something were to happen to her? *Lord,
You would never allow that, would You?* But suddenly
a horrible thought gripped me. There was another
mother somewhere who had asked God the same question. My knees felt weak. I couldn't put the thought of
this mother from my mind. Had she asked God, "How
can You let my innocent son go to prison?"

Immediately, I went downstairs to check Andrew. He
was okay. He looked so small, huddled in the middle of
his new junior bed, now that he had ceded his crib to
Elizabeth. I reached to stroke his cheek and hair . . . but
drew back my hand. I felt contaminated.

*Lord, please leave me alone. I know it's You who's
doing this to me. You must realize I can't do anything
about the past. Didn't You tell me in Your Word that all
my past sins were forgiven?*

The next day . . . the next week began my season of
tears. My eyes seemed as if they had been swollen and
red forever. I refused to look in the mirror and avoided
my reflection like an enemy. When I used the sink in the
downstairs bathroom, I kept my eyes lowered and
didn't even look into the small, round, foggy mirror
hanging above it on the wall.

I cried all day while David was at work. I cried every
time I looked at Elizabeth and Andrew because I feared
that my sin would be on their heads. I cried if I went for
a walk outside on the hard-packed snow. The tears froze
on my face. I cried while hanging wet laundry on lines
hung from the ceiling near the wood stove. I cried when
I thought of my church family and how they loved and
accepted me but didn't know the real me. I cried alone
. . . because I couldn't tell anyone.

This anxiety continued for months. Then, as was so
usual for me, I found myself convicted again out of
God's Word. One day I went to a women's Bible study

at a friend's house. The subject was restitution. I was nonplussed. I sat stone-cold and totally silent through the whole discussion.

After the session was over, I asked Bonnie, "Don't you think that sometimes Satan tempts us to make restitution for something in the past, but it really would only open up a can of worms? Don't you think that some things are better left alone? I mean, if a person has done something wrong and the Lord forgives him, don't you think that it could create unnecessary problems to go back and drag a bad situation up again?"

Her answer was casual but direct. "Will it restore something? Maybe that's the key."

Restore. Restore a tormented woman to God? A mother to her son? An imprisoned man to freedom? Yes, that's what my restitution could restore. But I couldn't. *Lord, I just can't.*

22

WINTER. I COULD barely concentrate. Not even house-work was satisfying or mind-occupying. I had to get out of the house. Often I'd pack the kids in the car and go driving to nowhere. I hated driving on icy roads, but I went. One day I warmed up our old 1973 Dodge and just headed out of our valley up over the Monadnock range. The road ran between white slopes dotted with dark clumps of conifers. The children were secure and sleeping, fastened into their car seats. The engine droned; I tried not to think.

Snow gathered and bracketed the windshield. "I can't face this thing, Lord. What about my children?" But doesn't the Bible say that the sins of the parents will be visited on the children? Would my children be deceivers: would Elizabeth be a liar? Would Andrew be disobe-dient to God? Because of me! But what if I went to jail? Wouldn't their lives be ruined as mine had been because of a motherless childhood?

The storm had broken now. Waves of white swept down from the mountains. My mind was storm-filled, too, with all I had learned in the last three years of being instructed by God and His Word. The verse that kept occurring to me then was Proverbs 19:5:

A false witness shall not be unpunished, and he that speaketh lies shall not escape.

I was afraid. Afraid of the chastisement of a just God. The Bible said the fear of the Lord was the beginning of wisdom. Was I learning wisdom? Obedience? Love? The car rocked in the wind. I remembered the words Jesus spoke to Peter:

> *Do you love Me?*
> *Yes, Lord, You know I love You.*
> *Do you love Me?*
> *Of course I love You, Lord. You know I love You.*
> *Do you really love Me, Cathy?*

> *"If ye love me, keep my commandments"*
>   *(John 14:15).*

I really wanted to love God and show Him that I loved Him. It was because He had shown His love to me first. In spite of the sin I couldn't face, He had provided for me and cared for my needs. With tears streaming down my face, I vowed, "Yes, Father, I will make this thing right. You have given me the desire, now please just give me the strength and courage that I will need."

David was waiting by the window when I turned the car into our driveway. The snow was filling the tracks of his borrowed truck and drifting against the house. The pines around the house were now completely covered white cones.

David rushed outside without his coat on. He untied the rope that fastened the wire gate, then came around to lift the sleeping children out of the car and into the house, one over each shoulder. I stamped my boots on the porch and went inside.

"You're home early," I said with feeling.

"The storm. I was worried about you. There's a traveler's advisory out."

"I must have missed it."

"When you drove in, the car lights were off. Are they working?"

"I think so. I must have forgotten to turn them on."

"Are you okay?"

"Sure."

He carried the kids to bed. He was such a sweet person. I wanted to be pleasant for his sake, but it was so hard to keep up a front. He came back and, seeing me still standing with my coat on by the door, he helped me off with it.

"Are you sure you're all right? That car's not safe in this weather."

"I'm all right. Have you had dinner?"

"A peanut butter and jelly sandwich. Come on, have a cup of coffee with me. Sit down."

I sat at the table and he went to the coffee maker and poured two mugs full of thick, black coffee that had been sitting on the hot plate for some time. He pulled up a chair.

"David, will you always love me?"

"Aha. Something *is* bugging you."

"No kidding. No matter what happens, will you still love me?"

"Yeah . . . no kidding." He forced a smile, but I could see that he was worried about me.

"You promise?"

"I promised once. And that was before I was a Christian. It goes double now . . . tell me what's bothering you, Cathy."

"Let's go upstairs." I took his hand. I just wanted to hold onto his hand. *Will you love me; will you?* He put his arm around me, and led me upstairs.

23

March 1985

I HAD THE desire to do what was right; I also had fears. It took time to gain strength and courage from the Lord, because I had no courage of my own. I was petrified because of my fear of losing David and the kids.

A few days later, another cold night . . . Wednesday, March 6. . . . I couldn't sleep. I put on my robe and slippers and went downstairs to flop in a chair and hug my Bible.

God's Word ministered to me powerfully that night. For He Himself said, "I will never leave you, nor forsake you, so that we can boldly say, 'The Lord is my Helper, I will not fear.' " He began to fill me with the strength and courage I had asked for. He wasn't just making me correct the evil I had done. He was going to help me do it. He was going to help me deal with the whole constellation of fears that possessed me: that everyone I knew would find out what I had done to an innocent man; that I would be hit with lawsuits or have to go to jail; that if the man in jail got out he might want to kill me; and paramount in my mind, the tormenting fear that David would leave me and take the children with him.

But I knew the time was now ripe and the Lord would enable me; with Him I could conquer my fears, if I would simply trust, obey, and do the will of the Father.

Thursday morning, March 7, I was talking with Bonnie Nannini on the phone, and the conversation came around to the subject of restitution. Immediately I became uptight and Bonnie, with typical sensitivity, picked up on my nervousness.

"Is there something you want to make up for, Cathy?" she asked gently.

I began to cry. "Yes, but I just can't tell anyone."

"You mean you can't tell David."

"No. Oh, no . . . Bonnie, they'll send me to jail. I'll lose David and my babies."

"You mean you committed a crime? When did this happen?"

"A long time ago. Eight years." I was gasping out the words now between sobs.

"You were a teenager then, Cathy. A juvenile. They won't send you to jail for anything you did as a minor, I'm sure."

"They will. You don't know what I did. I was horrible. I'm still horrible." I guessed she probably thought I had stolen a car, or been involved with drugs or something. Who would suspect the incredible thing I had done? It was not your typical teenage prank or crime. Nor would Bonnie suspect that I was in a sense still committing a crime, because my unconfessed lie kept a man in jail.

"You know that God has forgiven you, if you've prayed about it, Cathy. Does this situation really demand restitution? Can you restore something if you act?"

"Yes," I cried. "But I'm so scared."

"If you can't tell David, can you tell me?" I could just picture her pretty face drawn with sympathy and concern.

"No. I can't tell anyone."

"Then, Cathy, all I can do right now is pray for you.

You know I will. You know I'm here if you need me."
She was so comforting and kind. But I was still in limbo
. . . I had started to open up, but I couldn't get the truth
out. After I hung up, I rushed to my Bible to find
solace, courage, and some more st⁻ength to act. I didn't
want to block it out of my mind or run away this time.

Thursday night is our church's regular visitation
night. I was home alone, David was still at work, the
kids were getting ready for bed, and I was picking up
toys in Elizabeth's room. I thought, *If Bonnie would
just come over tonight, I think I could tell her, Lord. I
think I could get this awful thing off my mind, once and
for all.* At that very moment, the phone rang. It was
Bonnie.

"I've been praying, Cathy. I thought maybe I should
come by. Would you like me to come?"

"Yes . . . please." *This is my D Day*, I thought.

She was there in half an hour, during which time I got
the kids tucked away. She brought some magazines to
read, thinking that it might be a gentle way to lead up to
my problems. But I didn't want to pussyfoot around
now.

She opened her Bible to the Laws of Restitution in
Leviticus, but I told her I had already read them a thousand times.

"Bonnie," I said, "I'd better just tell you and get it
over with, but you're going to hate me."

"No, I won't," she said, touching my hand across the
table.

"Well, it was like this." Tears ran silently down my
face. "I accused a man of raping me eight years ago. It
was a lie; I was never raped. I was sixteen and having sex
with another boy." Her face registered no surprise. "I
thought he got me pregnant. I didn't know what to do.
You know I was living in a foster home then. I thought
they would get rid of me. They already knew that I had
been fooling around with boys and they'd warned me
about it. I knew they wouldn't put up with me if I was
pregnant. They'd send me to a State institution. And I

was just then doing well in school. I was planning for a
great big future. I was so confused. I was in a daze. So I
faked a rape.

"I figured if they thought some guy raped me,
then—well, they'd overlook the fact that I got pregnant.
They'd just feel sorry for me. So I ripped up my clothes
and cut myself up with a broken bottle and was going
home when some cops picked me up. I had made myself
up to look like I'd been raped and that's exactly what
they thought when they saw me. They took me to the
police station. One thing led to another. They asked me
to describe the rapist and made a sketch. Later they
showed me pictures of a guy who looked like the drawing. I told them that was the guy. I mean it looked so
obvious, they'd figure I was lying if I didn't say it was
him. Later, they picked him up and tried him and he
went to jail. He's been in jail for six years. He's in jail
right now. And I did it to him.

'See why I say I'm still horrible? See why I'm going
to go to jail? And why David's going to leave me. . . .'' I
started sobbing then. Bonnie had been calm and recep-
tive to everything I said. When I finished she got up and
came around the table; she put her arm around me and
started crying, too.

She stayed with me from half-past seven until eleven
o'clock at night. Before she left we knelt at the couch in
the living room and prayed together to know God's will
and do it. When we finally got up there were two wet
patches on the sofa from our tears.

But I'd broken through. I had told the truth about my
darkest secret. When I had first accepted Christ, I had
broken the pattern of lying that had become my way of
life. Now I had told the truth about a past sin that
demanded restitution. The truth, the Bible says, shall
make you free. I did, indeed, feel free . . . though I also
felt as vulnerable, weak and frightened as an infant taking her first step in the dark . . . but my Heavenly Father
was holding my hand.

Bonnie said she and Pastor would pray for me so I

would know how to do what I needed to do, and for the strength I would need in order to tell David. I found out later that they stayed up all night praying for me.

David came home from work at three in the morning. I had gone to bed, exhausted, but lay awake listening for the car in the driveway. He, too, was exhausted, so I decided to let him sleep and tell him in the morning.

I got up before him but didn't wake him until it was time for him to get ready for work again the next day. It was one o'clock Friday afternoon before he came down for breakfast. There was no turning back now. I had steeled myself and wasn't going to cry or anything. I just told him.

"David, I have to tell you something, but you're going to hate me. I just pray to God you won't leave me. You remember the rape. It never happened. I faked the rape because I was afraid I was pregnant by another guy. Then it just snowballed, and an innocent man went to jail because of me. But God wouldn't let me alone and now I'm finally telling the truth about it. I told Bonnie last night." At first he looked shocked, like the weight of a piano had just fallen on him. I couldn't imagine what was going through his mind about what I was like then and how I had lied to him for all these years. A marriage is built on trust . . . what must he be thinking of me? Outwardly he was calm and sweet as he always was. I knew he saw that I was totally distraught and he tried to reassure me.

"I love you, Cathy."

"No kidding, you're sure you love me even now?"

"What you did then doesn't change the way I feel about you now."

He told me he loved me. *He loved me.* He held me and hugged me and kept telling me not to worry. He loved me.

"But what should I do?"

"Cathy, you'll just have to do what's right."

We were sitting in the living room. After a while he had to go to work. He left at about 3:00 P.M., still telling

me he loved me. Through him God was giving me someone to lean on, though I was still unsure. When he went
out the door, I remember the exact words I said to myself, trying to harden my heart against my fears: *Well,
you can kiss this guy good-bye. He's never coming
back.*

Then I spent the whole day and night nervously
watching the clock. I stayed up in bed until three o'clock
the next morning. When David finally came to bed I just
melted into his arms, thanking God he had come back
to me.

24

THE EVENTS OF the next three months were so rapid, so unexpected, so confusing to me, that I should give a quick summary of what did happen.

I told Bonnie, Pastor Nannini, and David in early March. Pastor contacted a friend, John McLario, a respected Christian attorney in Menomonee Falls, Wisconsin. I called Mr. McLario on March 10. He asked me to describe in a letter the case and my reasons for coming forth at this time. I wrote and told him everything, giving him my Christian testimony, and he agreed to take the case. David and I sent him a small retainer, but as we would come to see, he did so much for us we could never repay him. He's been a Christian friend as well as a skillful attorney.

John made inquiries in Illinois. The case was reopened. The next major event was a hearing held in Judge Richard Samuels' courtroom in Cook County on April 4. By that time the press and TV had picked up the story, and what I had hoped would be a quiet, low-profile procedure to free Gary Dotson had become a media extravaganza. Judge Samuels' wood-paneled courtroom was as packed as a circus tent. Warren Lupel represented Gary Dotson and John stood by me. I told my story and was cross-examined by prosecutor Margaret Frossard.

On April 11, Judge Samuels denied Gary Dotson's petition, saying that he did not believe my recantation. Gary was returned to prison without bond.

After conferring with David and John, I decided that I still should do anything in my power to free Gary. I decided to accept every appropriate media opportunity to show my credibility and Gary's innocence. We were asked to appear on many TV programs. I was interviewed for an article for *People* magazine that, with editing, did not come out quite the way I had intended, and it hurt people now dear to me: Uncle Bill, Carol, and Bernie. There were broader issues to confront, too. We were asked to come to Washington to speak before a Senate subcommittee which was reviewing issues on juvenile justice.

Public outcry for Gary eventually brought Governor James Thompson into the picture. Though in his eight years in office Governor Thompson had never presided over a State Prisoner Review Board hearing, according to *Newsweek* magazine, he decided to preside over Gary's clemency hearing himself. It was held before five hundred spectators, most of them reporters, and a national cable TV audience. Some of the reporters called it "clemency under the big top." The governor stated the issue was that "the Illinois criminal justice system is being examined by the rest of the world." On the day before the hearing, his forty-ninth birthday, he displayed a T-shirt, a gift from his staff lawyers, which read, "Get Out of Jail Free" on the front, and on the back, "Go to Jail, Do Not Pass Go."

After three full days of testimony by various people involved in the case, the governor announced that he did not believe me. He believed Gary was guilty, but because he had served more time than most convicted rapists, his sentence would be commuted. Gary still carried the label of *felon;* neither his name nor his record was cleared. In essence he was on parole and any trivial violation could send him back to jail. He couldn't even leave Cook County without permission. This was not the freedom I had sought for him.

The personal experience of all those days was not quite so orderly. It was a time of extreme trial, when only God could comfort me.

25

At FIRST WE could muster only enough courage to tell our parents.

On March 18 David and I flew to Milwaukee to meet with the State Investigators who were going to interrogate me. Taking off from the Boston airport to Milwaukee, the plane banked and I looked out the window at the city. The blue, silvery harbor, with its black pattern of islands, grew smaller in the distance, and then we were lost in white.

John McLario met us at the airport in Milwaukee. I had envisioned an older businessman, but the man who met us at the airport was almost grandfatherly, with crinkly laughing eyes. He wore a suit and a gentleman's hat. He was warm and gracious and David and I immediately felt comfortable with him. He drove us to his office and we waited in the conference room for the investigators to come. I worked on my needlepoint as I waited. It had an intricate bouquet design, and I was making it for Carol's Christmas present. Five hours later, at four o'clock, the two men arrived. They looked huge to me, like football players. Their names were Hill and Katalinic. They took hardly any notes as they questioned me. I talked for about two hours and answered some very embarrassing questions.

Later John said to me, "Cathy, I think there may be

opposition to your recantation. You ought to know this so that you're prepared for it." I felt my heart thud. It had never dawned on me, never in my wildest imagination, in all those years I had hid the lie, that somebody would not believe me if I told the truth. I really believed that as soon as the case was opened they would see how I had lied. There was a man in prison whose freedom depended upon my telling the truth and being believed! Later I heard that one of the investigators had believed me that day but the other one didn't.

David's father picked us up in Milwaukee and drove us back to Chicago. I was afraid of what his reaction was going to be toward me when I told him about my recantation. I figured he'd be real quiet in the car and not know what to say, but in minutes he was talking and being his normal fun and affable self. "Teenagers do foolish things," was his only remark about the situation. We stopped and bought steak sandwiches to take home, and by the time we arrived in Homewood, I was assured that David's family would not reject me. They still loved me.

We left the next day, driving home in David's parents' new Escort. They planned to visit us in April around Easter, and they would pick up the car then. Sixteen hours later we were back home. It was wonderful. I had a lot of laundry to catch up on but before I began, David and I sat on the couch and prayed together. John 12:24 and 25 really spoke to us:

> *"Except a corn of wheat fall into the ground and die, it abideth alone: but if it die, it bringeth forth much fruit. He that loveth his life shall lose it; and he that hateth his life in this world shall keep it unto life eternal."*

Wednesday night we went to church for the midweek service and that morning an article about my recantation appeared in the newspaper. It had gone out all over the country. Almost everyone at the church knew, in-

cluding my friend Laura, who had spent the whole
afternoon crying out of shock. I figured everyone in the
church would hate me now. When Laura and her husband, Mike, walked into church, Laura came over to
me, looked at me, and gave me a hug. Mike hugged me,
too. All the church members immediately began to support us through action and prayer. Over the next three
months, they paid our mortgage and light bills; we were
constantly being handed money for travel expenses;
when we needed it, our children were lovingly taken care
of by an "aunt," "uncle," and "sister" whom they
knew well. Our house was cleaned by little elves, not
once but many times. Even our cupboards were jammed
full of food. Only a brother or sister in Christ could
have loved us the way they did.

My brother Steve gave me my first hint of what was to
come when he called and said somebody named Garza
from the Illinois State Prosecutor's Office was calling
him, as well as my grandmother, trying to find out what
was going on. Had my brother found out before I had a
chance to tell him? I would have to call everyone myself.
There were my friends, Liz and Lori. . . . My mother-in-
law called me the next morning just to tell me she loved
me. She said, "I just want you to know I love you. I
know this is going to be a hard experience for you but
Dad and I love you and we are behind you all the way."
Carol and Bernie were also supportive after their initial
shock wore off.

Warren Lupel sent an affidavit by regular mail to
John. John telephoned me and I went to the church to
type out the affidavit. Then I hurried to the Peterborough Library to have copies made, and then drove to
Deering to a notary public and mailed the documents
back to Warren Lupel by express mail. We didn't want
Dotson to stay in jail even one extra day.

"Gary Dotson." I hadn't said the name yet.

I had given an interview to a reporter from the
Milwaukee Sentinel. At one time during the interview,
Andrew fell down and I had to stop and pick him up
and comfort him. Because of demand I agreed to let

John set up a telephone conference with several newspaper reporters. The *Chicago Tribune* had been given and had printed false information from an "unnamed source close to the investigation" calling me a member of a cult, emotionally unstable, etc. We felt there was a need to answer these scandalous statements about my credibility. So there I sat on a stool at my kitchen counter, with the children running around right next to me. There must have been fifteen reporters on the line. After the interview, John told me I had been invited to appear on the "Today" show. He assured me I would be treated courteously and fairly (and I was). He emphasized that he would not tell me what to do, but that David and I would have to decide for ourselves. David and I prayed about it.

How public did we want to go with this thing? It seemed that public support would help Gary Dotson. I thought about how I had publicly demeaned him and taken six years of his life away from him. I remembered how in the Bible Zaccheus restored what he had stolen. I thought about what God had said about restoration in the Book of Leviticus. I realized that no matter what it cost me, I'd have to do all I could to free this innocent man. David agreed, and said he would stand with me and support me in any way he could. False and slanderous statements about my credibility were becoming more frequent in the news media, and that was a threat to Gary's freedom.

Finally, I called John and accepted the invitation to appear on TV. I hadn't wanted even my friends at church to know about this, and now it looked as if the whole world was going to be in on it. What frightened me more were reporters. It was obvious they could print anything at all and people would believe what they said.

The day we were to fly to New York, I was giving David a haircut at the kitchen table when a strange woman appeared at the door. Typical of David, he called, "Come on in!" It was a reporter from the *Chicago Tribune*.

We knew immediately she wasn't a Yankee. This

woman was definitely "city." I could tell by her dress and especially her shoes.

I said immediately, "I'm sorry, we're not talking to any reporters."

She began begging us for a story because she had come all this way and her editors were going to be really upset if she didn't come back with one. I said no, and then David chimed in with, "We're on our way to Boston."

"Oh? What are you going to do in Boston?"

"Well, actually, that's just where we catch a plane for—"

"David, I need to finish cutting your hair," I interrupted.

When we arrived at our hotel in New York, this same reporter was waiting at the elevator of our floor with a photographer.

I started shaking so badly, David practically had to hold me up. We finally were inside our room and I still couldn't stop shaking. John had warned us, "It's only the beginning; expect the worst. Be strong. Don't talk to anyone because what you say will be misconstrued. Remember, you're Christians, you're representing the Gospel. It's God who brought you forward with the truth in the first place."

The next day a story was printed in the *Chicago Tribune* that read:

> A reporter for the Tribune *met the twenty-three-year-old woman, Cathleen Crowell, Thursday in the small clapboard home where she lives with her husband and two small children in a rural New Hampshire town.*
>
> *"I'm not going to do anything that will jeopardize Gary's release," said the woman, now Cathleen Webb. "The only important thing is what happens to him."*
>
> *She said she was going to Boston with her husband, although it appeared that Boston was a stop on the way to New York City to talk about the case*

*on NBC-TV's "Today" show and ABC-TV's
"Good Morning America" program and other
television outlets. . . .*

The article was a long one, and quite involving. I marveled at how reporters put together stories.

Then I found out that I was going to be on the "Today" show on a split screen with Mrs. Dotson, who was
in a Chicago studio. I was scared. I wanted to roll up in
a ball and stay that way. How could I go through with
it? "David, I sent her son to prison for six years!" I was
crying. "How can I talk to her on TV? Oh, David, if I
had known about this before I got here, I don't think I
could have come." I said to myself, *I guess I'll have to
go through with it.* Then John told us "Good Morning
America" wanted us to be on that show, too. I nodded
quietly. Yes, I would do it.

At the hotel, I unpacked my toothbrush and night-
gown from the suitcase we had borrowed from friends
in the church, and climbed into bed. We read from the
Book of Acts in the Bible where the man with the weak
foot and ankle bones received strength to walk and leap
and praise God. I felt like that very person with the
weak feet and ankle bones. I needed God's strength to
stand up and do what was right. Only He could give me
the strength I needed to walk and leap in this recantation. David and I prayed together that night, "Dear
Lord Jesus, bless Gary Dotson and his family. Touch
them and restore to them what has been taken from
them. Only You can do it. You love Gary and it's because of Your love for him that You've brought this lie
to light. Please give him the joy and beauty of life that's
in You."

I wasn't walking and leaping yet.

The following morning a sea of reporters and cameras
were waiting for us at Rockefeller Center. Inside I was
shaking so badly I didn't think I could move my legs to
get out of the car. "Why do you suppose this is happening?" I tried to ask David, but the words wouldn't
come. I didn't want him photographed by the press. It

was my sin, not his. I didn't want him to have to pay for what I had done by being humiliated and disgraced in front of the whole nation.

John McLario and his wife, Lois, David, and I were led by Lisa Freed to the studio, but not without a struggle to get out of the car. It seemed as if reporters were pouring out of every crack in the sidewalk.

Of all the reporters we met during that ordeal, Jim Gibbons, an ABC reporter from Chicago, was the most gentlemanly. He flew to New York from Chicago with an entire crew to interview us. I was grateful to him because he was a most helpful person, instrumental in finding out the name *Gary Dotson*. I couldn't remember Gary's name, so John McLario called everywhere trying to find out who he was. I also didn't remember the date of the trial, so there wasn't much to go on.

Then we were finally in the studio and on camera. And I was confronting Mrs. Dotson. I could see and hear her over the monitor in the studio.

"I really want to say to Mrs. Dotson . . . that I'm so sorry . . . *Don't cry. Try to stay calm. You're on TV* . . . for what I did to you and your—*if you break down, you won't get out what you want to say!*—family and especially to Gary—I took six years away from him. I just really—*now she'll never respond to you. Why can't you say what you want to say clearly?* I just really want your forgiveness . . ." *Too late. I can't control it.* I started to cry ". . . especially Gary's forgiveness."

Mrs. Dotson said, "Don't worry, you're forgiven, Cathy. I just want my son back, and I thank you so much for coming forward. It took a lot of courage."

She was so gracious! This was more shocking to me than anything. In all my life I had never known what it was like to be soft or gracious. Now, after I had committed such a horrible wrong against a man and his family, I was on the receiving end of *their* graciousness and forgiveness.

"I wish I was wealthy," I stumbled, "I wish I had a million dollars I could give him to start his life over . . . but I don't. . . ."

Barbara Dotson, in her soft voice, said my confession was a gift from God.

More reporters, more cameras, people shouting questions: "How does it feel to hear the mother of a man you condemned tell you you're forgiven?" More television cameras, interviews: "Gary Dotson's life is worth more than my keeping silent and not telling the truth. I could not spend the rest of my life keeping silent." I knew that this was a terrible disgrace, but I remembered the words *Obedience is better than sacrifice* and I had to thank the Lord for giving me the grace to obey. No matter what the media did to me, Gary Dotson's freedom was worth it.

And the media attention had forced events. A hearing had been scheduled to review the Dotson case on April 4, 1985. Shortly before then, David and I, Bonnie, Pastor, and my children drove to Chicago in their small station wagon. After meeting John McLario and Gary Dotson's lawyer, Warren Lupel, on April 3, we began to prepare for the hearing before Judge Samuels.

26

Markham, Illinois
April 1985

ON APRIL 4, AFTER a breakfast of English muffins and
orange juice, David, John, and I headed for Markham
County Courthouse two hours early so we would beat
the reporters, in case they showed up.

When we pulled into the parking lot on 159th Street
and Kedzie, it was packed. Reporters, cameras, TV
trucks, lights everywhere. *Show no emotion,* I told
myself. "There are about a hundred and fifty yards of
stairs to get in the place," David warned.

". . . I can't," I whispered, pleading with David, but
he couldn't hear me. Reporters were swarming around
the car, cameras were aimed at the windows. Microphones were hanging over the door. It was then the
county deputies came out and escorted us in. They were
professional and forceful, and somehow we got up the
stairs.

Screaming, yelling, microphones, cameras . . . "What
if the judge sends him back to jail, Miss Crowell?"
"What if the judge doesn't believe you?" "What made
you do it?" "Mrs. Webb! Mrs. Webb!" *Thou wilt keep
him in perfect peace whose mind is staid on thee. . . .*
"How does it feel to send an innocent man to jail?"

Finally we were inside the small room adjoining the courtroom, where it was quiet.

Judge Richard Samuels, Circuit Court Judge, presides in Room 108 in the Markham court building. He is fifty-nine years old and was the same judge who presided over the original rape and aggravated kidnapping trial on May 22, 1979. He had already said, "It would be a rare event for a conviction to be overturned on recanted testimony."

Since this was a hearing, not a trial, there was no jury. The jury seats were filled with reporters. The courtroom was packed. I told my story the best I could, sometimes faltering, forgetting, praying. I faced a wall again. . . . Memory gone. Dates, times, what I said to whom eight long years ago.

Oh, Lord, I'm telling the truth now! Why is it so much harder for people to believe the truth? It seems they want to emphasize what I don't remember and ignore what I do remember. Why was it so easy to lie eight years ago?

I was supposed to go to South Suburban Hospital for tests and samples to verify the physical evidence in the case, but we were held up in the jury room off the courtroom for two and a half hours. John told us the delay was so the press wouldn't get to us, and we finally left by a side door where a deputy had told us to wait for him. He said he'd drive ahead of us to show us the way. We waited and he didn't show up so we left for the hospital on our own, thinking that after two and a half hours there wouldn't be any reporters still around.

John's car wasn't running well. It kept dying on us. Suddenly there were reporters everywhere. We finally pulled into the parking lot at the hospital after stalling several times along the way, and once there, we were again swarmed. It was raining and people were tugging at my sleeves, snapping pictures, sticking microphones in my face: "Do you have a message you'd like to give to today's American teenager?" "What do you think these new tests will prove?" "Why did you do it?" "Do you believe as a Christian that sex is inherently evil?"

"What do you think of your wife *now,* Mr. Webb?"

After the tests we finally were able to leave Chicago
for Menomonee Falls, and the reporters followed in
their cars. As we drove, the rain became worse, and before long it was raining huge chunks of hail. The next
time I looked back, instead of seeing a trail of cars with
reporters and photographers inside, I saw only a wall of
white hail. We had lost them. I sighed in relief, "The
hail must have come from the Lord. Can we eat lunch?
I'm starved."

We stopped at a roadside restaurant. Once seated, we
felt safe and began to relax somewhat. The waitress who
served us was friendly and she overheard us talking
about the Lord. Then she realized who we were. When
we left the restaurant, the parking lot was set up with
cameras, an entire film crew, plus the ever-present
reporters with their questions.

I missed the children, even though they were being
well taken care of by Grandma and Grandpa (David's
parents). I missed my home with the yellow daisies that
would be growing wild in our lazy, quiet pasture; the
oak and elm trees would be budding, and I could almost
hear the clucking of the chickens and the mooing of the
black-and-white cows in the field next door.

April 11, 1985

I did not testify that day, but waited in the jury room all
day. Nobody came to tell me what was going on; I was
trapped in there, worrying, praying, begging God to let
me out, let me testify, let me help! Sitting there alone,
not knowing what was going on, was horrible. I read the
magazines backward and forward, even the ads. There
was a puzzle on a table half put together, with scattered
pieces spread around. I hated puzzles. I didn't even have
my Bible for comfort.

Finally the court recessed for lunch. David, John,
Lois, Pastor, and Bonnie popped into the jury room. I
was so angry I couldn't speak. They recognized my dis-

tress and David vowed I wouldn't be left alone again.
Bonnie volunteered to sit with me during the afternoon
session. I loved Bonnie but I didn't want her to stay with
me. I wanted my husband. After a few hours I thought
of the words *I will not leave you comfortless,* and I
prayed that comfort for myself. Later, after all the
testimony was heard, I was ushered into the courtroom
and the decision was given by Judge Samuels:

> *Accordingly, from the evidence presented, I
> must regretfully find that the Petitioner has failed
> to sustain his burden, and I cannot find that per-
> jury was committed in 1979, and again, it is re-
> gretfully that I must deny the Petition and the
> judgment will stand.*

There was a gasp in the court. They nearly had to
carry me out of the building. I saw Gary Dotson's hand
come down on the table in anguish. I completely lost
control and broke down. I didn't care who saw me; I
didn't care what anybody thought. I sobbed, *"He's innocent! He's innocent! That man is innocent!"* as we
left the court building. The thought of Gary going back
to prison was devastating to me.

Judge Samuels said in his ruling that the law takes a
jaundiced view of recanted testimony.

Nick Howell, a spokesman for the Illinois Department of Corrections, said that 124 persons who were
convicted of rape in Cook County were released from
prison in 1983 after serving an average of 4.5 years.
Gary Dotson had already served 6 years behind bars,
longer than most offenders convicted of rape in Cook
County.

Judge Samuels left the Markham County Courthouse
with a police escort that day.

Gary Dotson walked up the ramp to the prison in
handcuffs and leg irons.

Alan Dershowitz, a Harvard law professor, told the
Chicago Tribune:

* * *

*To look suspiciously on recanted testimony is
simply a way of saying that we will allow injustice
to continue. The one thing we know for sure is that
the main witness against him is capable of telling
very convincing lies. The first time she convinced a
judge, a jury, and a lot of people, and the second
time she also convinced a great many people. It is
incontrovertible that she is capable of telling convincing lies, and that alone should result in a new
trial where a group of jurors could determine which
is a lie and which is truth.*

27

WE CONTINUED TO use every means at our disposal to get Gary out. I took a lie detector test on April 14 to show that I was now telling the truth. [*See* Appendix A.] New evidence was brought forth now because of the tests made on April 4. It turned out that the forensic testimony in the 1979 trial by forensic expert Timothy R. Dixon was now proven *false*. Rob Warden, editor of the newspaper *Chicago Lawyer,* said that the latest evidence from the new tests indicated Dixon's testimony was "patently false and the jury was seriously misled" at the first trial, which sent Dotson to prison. Dotson's public defender did not even challenge Dixon's evidence at the 1979 trial. Edward Blake, one of the nation's leading forensic scientists, called Dixon's testimony misleading. Another forensic expert, Mark Stolorow, also produced results that contradicted Dixon's trial testimony of 1979. The new tests proved that the semen found in the panties worn on July 9, 1977, could belong to 66 percent of the white male population and 78 percent of the black male population, quite a difference from Dixon's testimony that Dotson's semen type was shared by only 10 percent of the population.

Later the *Chicago Lawyer* also supported its claim by featuring a four-page article in its June 1985 issue which included a lengthy interview with Charles P. McDowell. [*See* Appendix B.]

McDowell is chief of the Special Studies Division of the Directorate of Investigative Analysis of the United States Air Force's Office of Special Investigations in Washington, D.C.

McDowell's opinion that the rape accusation was false is based on his comparison of various details of my 1979 testimony with a model he developed to help investigators recognize false allegations.

The model is based on an Air Force study of 1,218 rape accusations—of which 460 were classified as proven, 212 were classified as false, and 546 were classified as unresolved.

He stated the scratches on my abdomen—superficial marks that appeared to form letters or words—are perhaps the single most important indication that I was lying. Scratches that appeared to form letters or words were seen in several of the false accusation cases studied by the Air Force. However, the phenomenon was not seen even once in a legitimate case. [*See* Appendix B.]

After the decision of April 11, Judge Samuels was given round-the-clock police protection. Some people believed him to be biased because he had been the original judge on the case. Judge Samuels said he entered the proceedings with his mind wide open. He said he "felt sorry for [Dotson's family]. I personally felt sorry for Dotson." The judge began to receive hate mail and threats on his life. I felt responsible for it all. I only wanted to come forward and confess my lie. Then I expected to go to jail for perjury. It had never occurred to me that I wouldn't be believed. I was not aware of the precedents and statistics about false recantations that Judge Samuels used against me. In fact, later Rob Warden would point out in the May 1985 issue of *Chicago Lawyer* that, of the five cases cited by Judge Samuels, one did not even involve recantation and the other four weren't a *victim's* recantation.

The next step could only be to appeal to the governor. On April 19, Warren Lupel, Dotson's lawyer, petitioned the governor and the Illinois Prisoner Review Board for an Executive Clemency Hearing. Lupel also appealed Judge Samuels' ruling and asked for Dotson's release on bond, but on April 24, the Appellate Court refused bond. Dotson stayed put, having been moved to the Dixon Correctional Facility for his own safety. He was depressed and given sedatives. On April 26, Lupel went to the Illinois Supreme Court to appeal, and on May 1, the Supreme Court released Gary Dotson on $100,000 bond.

28

Illinois Prisoner Review Board Executive Clemency Hearing May 1985

THE ILLINOIS STATE BUILDING is an imposing building. It has been described as a "seventeen-story pie wedge" and "an inverted teacup made of mirrored glass." Walking past the orange pillars and entering the strange glass-domed interior on May 9, I couldn't look up to see the sun glaring through every prism of glass onto the black-and-white mosaic sundial patterns on the floor. I kept my head still, my eyes straight ahead. *Show no emotion.*

Gary Dotson must be nervous. I wished he had the Bible I had brought for him. Earlier there had been no appropriate time to present it to him. Even though he might not have realized it, I knew he must be in need of comfort from the Living Word. I arranged for my mother-in-law to give it to Barbara Dotson at the end of the last day of testimony (which she did). We did not want the news media to run wild and print slanted and patently false information, claiming I had come forward just to proselytize and convert Gary Dotson. True believers know that only God, in the form of the Holy

Spirit, is able to convert man unto Him, but it was doubtful the media would understand that.

I was nervous, too. I feared I would be charged with perjury by the Illinois judicial system, which many felt I had made look foolish. When I left New Hampshire for the clemency hearing, I didn't know whether I would be returning. The week before I left, I was sitting next to David in church when the choir sang a song that was like a soothing balm to my soul. I put my head on David's shoulder and cried. I really needed that release, and God knew it. Later I found out that the choir members couldn't look at me, for fear they also would burst into tears as they sang these words:

> *God never moves without purpose or plan*
> *When trying his servant and molding a man.*
> *Give thanks to the Lord*
> *Though your testing seems long;*
> *In darkness He giveth a song.*
> *O rejoice in the Lord. He makes no mistake.*
> *He knoweth the end of each path that I take. . . .*

The hearings were televised for all the world to see. Why, I still can't understand. Why would the governor of a state take part in such a show? The little theater of a makeshift court was set up in a room behind a restaurant on the first floor. David and I stayed in the Bismarck Hotel a block away. It was, oddly enough, across the street from the restaurant where I had seen my father the day I invited him to my wedding.

Warren Lupel made eleven points on behalf of his client at the clemency hearing. [*See* Appendix C.] He was given a round of applause when he concluded. On May 12, 1985, Governor Thompson granted Gary Dotson a commutation of sentence, which meant he was a free man.

Free, but not pardoned. What the governor did was to concede Dotson had served enough time for his crime, without finding that he was not guilty. On his record he was still a convicted felon.

29

New York
May 14, 1985

GARY DOTSON AND I agreed to appear on the "Today" show together. The evening before the show, we met in a hotel room with David, Warren Lupel, and John McLario. It was a short meeting, but I did ask Gary whether he had received a Bible from me, since by that time I had been told he had received numerous Bibles.

"Look through it sometime," I told him. "It's what got you out of prison." The conversation quickly turned to other matters, and the next day we appeared on the morning TV shows.

David and I flew back to New Hampshire. Looking down at the city from the airplane, New York became a tiny checkerboard of toy buildings and concrete; it looked like a strategic board game to me. Clouds overtook us.

I thought how our lives would never be the same but how thankful I was that God had broken through impenetrable walls and shown mercy to Gary Dotson.

Fear thou not, for I am with thee; be not dismayed, for I am thy God; I will strengthen thee; I will help thee; yea, I will uphold thee with the right hand of my righteousness.

The words of Laura Dotson, Gary's sister, came to me as I removed my shoes to give my feet a rest. "Cathy, I just want to thank you for what you've done for my brother. You've given him a second chance at life. Thank you for coming forward and telling the truth."

I turned my face to the airplane window. *Oh, God, how could one person bring so much suffering to others? The Dotson family could curse me, hate me, plan vengeance against me, and yet—they were able to forgive me. Thank You, Lord.*

I hoped that my story would demonstrate how destructive lies can be—to the innocent, and also to the liar. I hoped it would show one thing more—there is an alternative to a life of lies. Those who open themselves to the grace and presence of the living God can have their motives, goals, ideas, drives, thoughts, and behavior transformed.

God hates lying, the Bible says. He proclaims Himself as Truth. In knowing Him, the truth becomes the alternative choice for the liar. I was once motivated by fear—of being found out, being exposed, being hurt, being accused, being mistreated, being cast away, being unacceptable, and the worst fear, the fear of just disintegrating and being lost. It wasn't until I allowed myself to be washed clean from inside out by a Spirit greater than mine, the Holy Spirit, that I was freed from fear.

The Bible says, "If any man be in Christ he is a new creature; behold old things are passed away, all things have become new."

There were a few more battles to fight on Gary's behalf, but I was already looking forward to a new life with my husband, my family, my church, and my God.

In August 1985 Gary Dotson's attorney lost a bid to have a reexamination of the physical evidence (blood, hair, and saliva) from the 1979 trial. Jack Rimland, the defense attorney, said that new tests could show that Dotson did not have intercourse with Cathy Webb. Judge Richard J. Fitzgerald of the Criminal Court denied the motion. A bid for a new trial was also later denied.

The fascination with the Webb/Dotson case continues to make headlines. Articles in publications as diverse as *Moody Monthly, Redbook,* and *Playboy* appeared in September and October. Other media interest in the story is strong, and reportedly a book from Gary Dotson's perspective is planned.

Gary Dotson continues to reside in the Chicago area. Cathy and her family live in New Hampshire. She is expecting her third child in February 1986.

Appendix A

On April 14, 1985, Cathy Webb willingly submitted to a lie detector test. Here is a portion of the results of that test, as well as the results of Gary Dotson's test of May 6, 1985. He also was willingly tested.

(1) On July 9, 1977, were you physically with Gary Dotson?
   Answer—NO   Opinion—TRUTHFUL

(2) On July 9, 1977, did you take part in a sex act with Gary Dotson?
   Answer—NO   Opinion—TRUTHFUL

(3) On July 9, 1977, the night you said you were raped, did you have any physical contact with Gary Dotson?
   Answer—NO   Opinion—TRUTHFUL

(4) On July 9, 1977, did you take part in a sex act with anyone?
   Answer—NO   Opinion—TRUTHFUL

(5) Had you physically seen Gary Dotson before you viewed him in the police lineup?
   Answer—NO   Opinion—TRUTHFUL

(6) On Thursday, April 4, 1985, did you tell any lies before Judge Richard L. Samuels?
   Answer—NO   Opinion—TRUTHFUL

(7) On Thursday, April 4, 1985, did you give any

false testimony under oath before Judge
Richard L. Samuels?
Answer—NO   Opinion—TRUTHFUL

(8) On Thursday, April 4, 1985, did you pur-
posely withhold any information while under
oath before Judge Samuels, about what
truthfully happened to you on July 9, 1977?
Answer—NO   Opinion—TRUTHFUL

(9) Have you been offered or promised anything
by anyone to change your testimony about
Gary Dotson sexually assaulting you?
Answer—NO   Opinion—TRUTHFUL

(10) Have you received anything from anyone to
change your testimony about Gary Dotson
sexually assaulting you?
Answer—NO   Opinion—TRUTHFUL

Gary Dotson's Responses:

(1) Do some people call you Gary?
Answer—YES Opinion—TRUTHFUL

(2) Are you more than twenty-one years old?
Answer—YES Opinion—TRUTHFUL

(3) On July 9, 1977, were you physically with
Cathy Crowell Webb?
Answer—NO   Opinion—TRUTHFUL

(4) Are you in Chicago right now?
Answer—YES Opinion—TRUTHFUL

(5) On July 9, 1977, did you take part in a sex act
with Cathy Crowell Webb?
Answer—NO   Opinion—TRUTHFUL

(6) Did you ever force anyone to have sex with
you?
Answer—NO   Opinion—TRUTHFUL

(7) Did you ever go to school?
Answer—YES Opinion—TRUTHFUL

(8) On July 9, 1977, did you force Cathy Crowell
Webb to have sexual intercourse with you?
Answer—NO   Opinion—TRUTHFUL

(9) On July 9, 1977, did you ejaculate on or in Cathy Crowell Webb?

Answer—NO   Opinion—TRUTHFUL

(10) Had you physically seen Cathy Crowell Webb before your preliminary hearing on this case?

Answer—NO   Opinion—TRUTHFUL

Appendix B

The following is an edited text of the interview between Charles P. McDowell and Rob Warden of the *Chicago Lawyer* (June 1985):

Warden: *Do you believe the account of the rape that Cathleen Crowell Webb gave under oath at Gary Dotson's trial in 1979?*

McDowell: No, I don't believe it. . . .

Warden: *Weren't all the cases of this type you studied reported to authorities?*

McDowell: Yes, but not initially. One of the features that we found to be common in false allegations is that they are rarely made initially to authorities. What usually happens is that a "victim" tells a relative or friend that she's been raped, and this third party will notify the authorities.

Warden: *Cathleen Webb claims that she didn't plan to tell the police she had been raped, but that police just stumbled onto her accidentally. Is that a factor in why you don't believe her 1979 testimony?*

McDowell: It's a factor, but it's not very significant by itself. No one feature by itself is diagnostic. The significance is where these things co-occur. Any one feature in our model may be found in actual rapes. . . .

Warden: *What are the common features that you've seen in false accusations?*

McDowell: There are a dozen in all, but I think two are the most important. First, the false accusation is always instrumental. It solves a problem from the "victim's" perspective. It may explain a pregnancy or venereal disease or otherwise conceal evidence of promiscuity. It may assuage guilt or enable the false accuser to avoid responsibility for her acts. It may exact revenge. The point is that the false accusation invariably serves some purpose. A genuine rape usually does not. On the contrary, it often creates a serious problem for the victim.

Second, and I think this is the most important area, the physical injuries of false victims are usually superficial—minor cuts, scratches, or abrasions. Although they may appear to be extensive, they don't amount to much. The cuts and scratches virtually never cross the eyes, the lips, the nipples, or the vagina proper. You typically see a peculiar hatching or cross-hatching effect in the scratches. What happens here is that the false victim scratches herself but does not immediately see a welt. She thinks she must not have done it hard enough, so she does it again. She applies another scratch coming from a slightly different direction. By the time the welts began to appear, you get this hatching. You do not see that in legitimate rape cases. . . .

Here are Charles McDowell's findings:

THE AIR FORCE MODEL OF A FALSE RAPE ACCUSATION	CATHLEEN CROWELL WEBB'S 1977-1979 RAPE ACCUSATION
Physical injuries of false accusers usually are limited to superficial cuts, scratches, and abrasions. Scratches often appear in a hatching or cross-hatching pat-	The physical injuries found on Webb's body on the night of July 9, 1977, were entirely superficial. They consisted primarily of scratches on her abdomen, some

tern, due to repeated attempts to make the scratches visible. Scratches that resemble letters or words sometimes are found on false accusers—typically on the abdomen—but are not found on actual victims.

False accusers frequently claim that they offered vigorous and continuing physical resistance but suffered no serious reprisals. Most actual rape victims do not offer vigorous and continuing resistance, and those who do often suffer extremely brutal reprisals.

A false accusation typically solves some perceived problem for the "victim." It may, for instance, explain a pregnancy or venereal disease, or it may exact revenge. In contrast, actual rapes seldom appear to solve a problem. Actual rapes usually create serious problems.

False accusers usually do not make their allegations initially to authorities. Typically they make the allegations to friends or relatives who in turn inform the authorities.

False accusers, more often than legitimate victims, claim to have been raped by strangers.

False accusers typically claim to have been attacked by multiple assailants and/or that the assailant(s) fit an extremely unsavory stereotype.

False accusers, more often than

of which appeared to form words or letters. Assistant State's Attorney Raymond Garza, in his closing argument to the jury at Dotson's 1979 trial, contended that the scratches spelled "Love" and "Hate."

Webb testified at Dotson's 1979 trial she scratched her rapist's chest and ears with her fingernails. "I tried to fight him off," she said, "and I couldn't." When asked on cross-examination what her attacker's response was, she said, "He just grabbed my hand."

Webb testified on April 4, 1985, that she invented the story that she had been raped because she feared that she was pregnant as a result of a consensual sexual encounter. She said she feared that if she was pregnant her guardians might kick her out of the house.

Webb testified on April 11 and May 9, 1985, that she originally intended to tell her false story only to her foster parents, but told it to police when they picked her up by chance.

Webb told police on the night of July 9, 1977, and later, that her rapist was a stranger.

Webb claimed that her rapist had long, greasy, stringy hair, looked "burned out," and that he and his accomplices were drinking beer and snorting something.

Webb claimed on July 9, 1977,

legitimate victims, claim to have been victims of "blitz" rapes—simple penile insertions with no collateral sexual activity. Actual rapes frequently entail collateral activity—fellatio, cunnilingus, or anal sodomy.

and subsequently to have been the victim of a blitz-type rape that consisted of a simple penile insertion with no fellatio, cunnilingus, anal sodomy, or other collateral sexual activity.

False accusers, far more frequently than actual victims, tend to be vague on details. When a false victim does provide details, she often does so with a relish that real victims seldom have.

Webb testified in 1979 that she was abducted and held for two hours, but she was not asked to account for what happened during the period other than the rape.

False accusers, far more frequently than actual victims, cannot say exactly where the alleged rape occurred.

Webb claimed the rape occurred in a moving car and that her view of the outside was restricted throughout the incident.

In false accusation cases, far more frequently than in legitimate cases, the purported crime scene and the physical evidence are found to be inconsistent with the allegation.

There are several inconsistencies between Webb's original story and the physical evidence. For instance, how did mud get onto her clothing if the rape occurred in a car?

More often than actual victims, false accusers claim to have received telephone calls or other contact from their "rapists" before or after the alleged crime.

Webb did not claim to have received calls but, according to the testimony of others, claimed after the purported rape that one of her abductors came into the restaurant where she worked.

False accusers, more often than legitimate victims, have personal problems, including difficulty in interpersonal relationships and a history of lying and exaggeration.

Webb's foster mother, Carol Smith, has testified that Webb had a history of lying. Webb told of her difficulties in interpersonal relationships in a by-lined article in the April 29, 1985 issue of *People*.

Appendix C

Here is a summary of the eleven key points in Warren Lupel's summation at the May 1985 Illinois State Prisoner Review Board clemency hearing. These eleven points were errors, he claimed, in the 1979 trial.

1. Five persons testified before the Grand Jury in open court in 1979 that Gary Dotson was nowhere near the scene of the "rape." (Five witnesses are usually enough to establish credibility).
2. Gary's mother testified that the clothing described by Miss Crowell was not like any owned by her son; nor did he own a white belt.
3. New forensic evidence shows the semen stains could belong to two-thirds of the white male population and 78 percent of the nonwhite population, as opposed to original *false* evidence that only 10 percent of the population, of which Gary was one, possessed semen of that type.
4. *One* pubic hair—which was said to resemble Gary's—is not sufficient evidence.
5. Prosecutor Garza claimed that Cathy Crowell was a virgin. She was not a virgin on July 9, 1977.

6. There was improper prosecutorial conduct when Prosecutor Garza told the jury that Dotson's five witnesses were liars.

7. Cathy described in detail the car in which she said she was kidnapped, but *the car didn't exist*. No car was ever found.

8. Cathy said her attacker bit her breasts—but there were no teeth marks on her breasts, only nail marks.

9. She said she scratched and gouged her attacker on the chest and behind the ears, but when Gary Dotson was arrested six days later, his body was clean of scratches.

10. There are opposing interpretations of drawings on her stomach. Why were the lines on her stomach all straight if she was trying to ward off an attack?

11. Cathy described her attacker as a man *without* a mustache. Dotson had a dark mustache at the time of his arrest. The photo of him in the police book with a light mustache and long hair was taken three years previously, when he was seventeen years old. On July 9, 1977, he was twenty years old.

27 million Americans can't read a bedtime story to a child.

It's because 27 million adults in this country simply can't read.

Functional illiteracy has reached one out of five Americans. It robs them of even the simplest of human pleasures, like reading a fairy tale to a child.

You can change all this by joining the fight against illiteracy.

Call the Coalition for Literacy at toll-free **1-800-228-8813** and volunteer.

Volunteer Against Illiteracy. The only degree you need is a degree of caring.